Materials

for Inspirational Design

Chris Lefteri

RotoVision

Contents

Materials

for Inspirational Design

A RotoVision Book
Published and distributed by RotoVision SA
Route Suisse 9
CH-1295 Mies
Switzerland

RotoVision SA
Sales & Editorial Office
Sheridan House, 114 Western Road
Hove BN3 1DD, UK

Tel: +44 (0)1273 72 72 68
Fax: +44 (0)1273 72 72 69
Email: sales@rotovision.com
www.rotovision.com

10 9 8 7 6 5

ISBN-13: 978-2-940361-50-2
ISBN-10: 2-940361-50-9

Book design by Fineline Studios
Art direction by Tony Seddon

Reprographics in Singapore by
ProVision Pte. Ltd.
Tel: +656 334 7720
Fax: +656 334 7721

Printed in Singapore by Star Standard Industries (Pte.) Ltd.

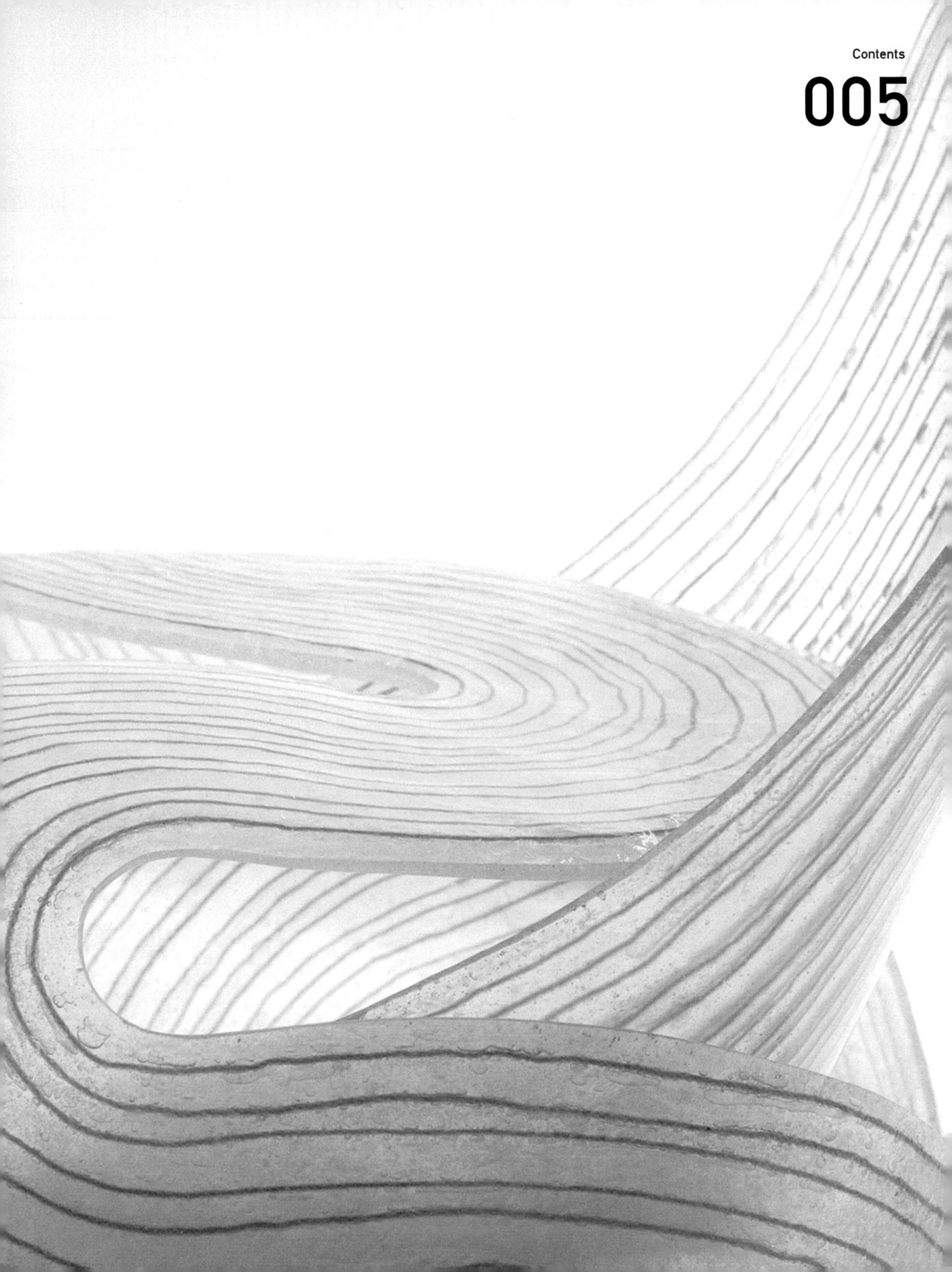

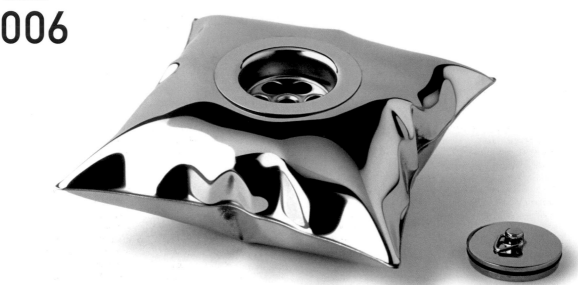

Introduction

The world of materials is a diverse place, with more available to us today than ever before. Here you will see just a sample of the many products and processes involving ceramics, glass, metal, plastic, and wood. The purpose of this book is to provoke you into questioning and thinking about a selection of what are some of the most interesting, original, and sometimes just plain fun materials in the world.

Ceramic is a wonderful material; malleable and pliable, it can be pushed and pulled, squeezed, molded, poured, and ground. It can be immediate and simple to form, but at the same time it can be highly precise and shockingly hard, with the most enduring of physical properties. It can be played with in the school art class, but it is also used in incredibly advanced applications and applied in extreme environments like a space shuttle. It can be polished to an extraordinarily smooth surface but it is also appreciated for its rough surface texture. Unsurprisingly, most people immediately imagine mugs, plates, bowls, and cups when they think of ceramics. It seems to be the best hard-wearing, long-lasting, and hygienic material for dinnerware, with no other materials in line to take its place. These products of function and adornment also take advantage of the unique ability of ceramics to form an alliance with a painted, glassy skin, creating a decorative and hard surface. It is this attribute that allows the same product to be sold with several different surfaces. These humble products represent an everyday application for ceramic, but one that can also be beautiful, ornamental, and personal.

Modern uses of glass are a great example of the evolving science of materials. The discovery of a new formulation of glass paved the way for the development of fiber optics, but it was the ability to manipulate this 7,000-year-old material and form it into ultra-thin, flexible strands capable of carrying light over several miles that really developed our methods of communication. Other more everyday inventions also owe their popularity to the manufacturing technology used to process them. Thomas Edison's tungsten lightbulb was a remarkable development—however, it cannot be separated from the process of forming millions of lightbulbs cheaply and efficiently. The invention of glassblowing, which, in terms of the history of glass is relatively new, was a milestone in production. It has since been used to produce a multitude of products. The sense of wonder in glass is not so much in the material itself, but more in how we have adapted and applied it in so many areas and how it exists in ways you would never have imagined.

About three quarters of the elements in the periodic table are metals, about half of which are commercially important. From this relatively small number of elements, we have managed to cook up at least 10,000 varieties of alloys. Metals are in the air we breathe, the food we eat, and the packaging around it; we live and work in metal buildings, we travel in metal containers, and we wear metals on our bodies; metals are in our water and in our soil. We are closer to metals than any other material; metals are in our blood. We exploit metals in so many different ways yet how often do we really look at them? Without a doubt, most of us take their extraordinary benefits for granted, and when we do appreciate them, it can often be distorted by the monetary value we have imposed upon them. We forget that metals come from the earth, and we are largely ignorant of the processes that metals go through, and the hardships that people endure for our everyday benefit. Metals will always engage and fascinate us with their strength, versatility, and inherent beauty, yet we are desensitized and conditioned not to question the intrinsic properties of these raw materials. I hope this book will go some way to redress the balance and inspire new ideas of exploring this most ancient and precious of materials.

For designers, plastic is an infinitely adaptable material, which easily takes on complex shapes—a material with the potential to be squeezed, pulled, injected, foamed, and sandwiched. Plastic epitomizes mass-production and low cost, while also being a material of "infinite transformation." But some of the strongest additions to the family of plastic materials are from the area of ecological plastics. Plastics that are not only derived from rapidly renewable sources, but are also biodegradable and compostable. Here the definition of plastics is shifting from being the environmental criminal to a material that comes from nature and returns to nature. With these new materials manufacturers are, for the first time, having to think about how to unmake the products

that they have become so efficient at making. This book illustrates and presents a number of producers internationally who are making biopolymers from agricultural products, such as starch-based vegetables, like corn.

Wood has an ability to bring out the designer in all of us. It's so accessible and easy to manipulate, it cries out to be shaped, carved, scratched, sanded, and nailed. Wood is one of the most widely understood materials; everyone can name at least a few different types. Oak, beech, and teak, for example, are part of the language of consumerism and products are sold on the basis of their varying qualities. Most of us, at some point in our consumerist lives, will choose a specific wood for that new living-room floor or dining-room table. Wood appears in countless forms: charcoal, building materials, cooking utensils, the book you are holding at this moment! It has to be one of the most used (and abused) materials available to us. It fulfills so many familiar functions in our daily lives that it often goes unnoticed. Yet the humble tree is a miracle of nature.

To be drawn into the traditions and values that it suggests, without considering the ugly side of modern wood production, is irresponsible. Unfortunately, wood is not unique in generating the greed and disrespect that go hand in hand with the love of any object or substance of desire. Large-scale deforestation and the destruction of massive areas of natural habitat and beauty continues in the name of profit and progress. However, the aim of this book is not to debate the complicated pros and cons of using materials, but instead to present a range of products, materials, and methods of production. Like all materials, the use of wood has its down side: yes, there is waste and, yes, a valuable natural resource is being depleted, but within these pages you will find examples where both these issues have been addressed through finding intelligent and alternative uses for what would usually be considered waste material. It is not too late for us to recognize and take steps toward a sustainable timber industry. Through well-managed and sustainable forests it is possible to produce wood for many uses. Wood commands too much respect to be in or out of fashion. Trees have one of the longest lifespans of all living forms—our oldest living trees are 5,000 years old. Wood was here long before we were and, if managed with the respect our natural resources deserve, will be here long after we are gone.

009 Ceramics

010

Silky smooth

Want to leave your skin feeling silky smooth? Then why not try some boron nitride in your makeup? Although used in small quantities, typically between three and 10 percent is added to cosmetics. This ingredient offers a soft, elegant feel with good skin adhesion, while providing various optical features.

But this is a material that, in different grades, offers a range of contradictory applications. Together with diamond and silicon nitride, cubic boron nitride is one of the hardest materials around and is superb for cutting tools.

There are two types of this material: hexagonal boron nitride, which has high temperature applications similar to graphite and is known for its soft and lubricious qualities; in contrast, cubic boron nitride is renowned for its hardness and its use for cutting, grinding, and drilling.

Key Features	**Silky feel**
	Excellent adhesion
	Can be tailored and applied to a range of products
	Has a nontransfer property
	Good lubrication
	Chemically inert
	Nontoxic
More	**www.debid.co.uk**
	www.bn.saint-gobain.com
	www.acccos.com
Typical Applications	**High-purity powders are used in cosmetics like foundations, lipsticks, pencils, etc. Its good lubrication qualities make it useful for minimizing friction in a variety of materials and industrial production methods.**

**Cosmetics with particles
of hexagonal boron nitride
Manufacturer:
Saint-Gobain**

Tough

Zirconia is a commonly used high performance ceramic. Used over alumina because it is tougher and more resistant to cracking, its particles are small, which gives it a sleek surface finish suitable for products such as blades, pistons, bearings, and even luxury jewelry.

Most watchmakers use more conventional materials for their timepieces—steel, plastic, brass, gold—but not Rado. Since the Rado brand was first launched in 1957, the Swiss watchmaker has built a reputation for its unique application of advanced materials.

In a short period of time, Rado established the world's first scratchproof watch, their aim being, "To make watches that are beautiful and stay beautiful." It was in the 1980s that ceramics were first used as part of their assortment of high-performance materials. By this time, ceramics had already proved themselves in a range of technical applications like space shuttles. This offered Rado the possibility to produce an extremely hard, scratch-resistant material that would live up to their aim.

Ultra-fine zirconium oxide or titanium carbide powder is used for the ceramic watches. These powders are pressed into shape and sintered at a temperature of 2,642°F (1,450°C). The components are then polished with diamond dust to achieve the ultra-shiny, metallic surface. The company also use ceramic injection molding for the Ceramica range, which allows for the production of intricate, complex forms. The colors are achieved by using ultra-pure, high-melting-point color oxides that are mixed with the ceramic powder to enable color variations.

**Sintra Chronograph
ceramic watch
Manufacturer: Rado**

Dimensions	**Watch face: 34mm x 32mm**
Key Features	**Excellent strength and fracture toughness**
	Very hard and wear-resistant
	Good chemical-resistance
	High temperature capability up to 4,352°F (2,400°C)
	Dense
	Low thermal conductivity (20 percent that of alumina)
More	**www.rado.com**
Typical Applications	**As well as being used in these watches, its smooth and fine surface finish combined with its toughness makes zirconia an ideal ceramic for cutting blades and kitchen knives. It is also used in car oxygen sensors which use a form of electrically conductive zirconia. Other applications include medical prostheses and pump seals and valves.**

012

Heat beating

The ceramics used on the Orbiter space shuttle tiles are excellent at dissipating heat so that, in a domestic scenario, within seconds of taking a tile from an oven, you could hold it on one of its edges while the center would be glowing red.

The use of ceramics on the Orbiter is a unique application of an ancient material in a product of the future. The tiles thermally protect the shuttle from temperatures between −249°F (−156°C) cold in space to the 3,000°F (1,649°C) burning heat of reentry.

This ability to withstand thermal shock is demonstrated by the fact that you could take a tile out of a 2,300°F (1,260°C) oven and immerse it in cold water without damage. As a result of this excellent thermal stability gaps of 25mm to 65mm need to be left between the tiles and the shuttle to take account of the movement which takes place in the Orbiter's metal structure.

Dimensions	30mm–125mm
Key Features	**Near zero thermal expansion**
	Exceptionally good thermal shock-resistance
	Good chemical inertness
	Lightweight approximately 93 percent porosity
More	**www.lockheedmartin.com**
	www.accuratus.com
Typical Applications	**The technology used on the tiles has been used on Earth to produce vacuum-like insulation for refrigerators, furnaces, and catalytic converters.**

High-temperature reusable surface insulation tiles for the space shuttle Developed by: Ames Research Center, Mountain View, California, US Manufacturer: Lockheed Missiles and Space Division

When you want to cut a piece of glass you scribe it before applying pressure and snapping it in half. The reason this works is that you are introducing a flaw in the surface, which opens up when you apply any tension. This same principle explains why ceramics are not very good under tension. But, as with all materials, ceramics can defy expectations: through a process called transformation, toughening the ceramic material can make it flexible.

The weakness in ceramics comes from the pores or gaps in the material. The reason that metals, for example, are tough is because of their ability to plastically deform. The nature of bonding of the atoms in ceramics makes them hard and strong, but it also stops them from plastically deforming. By reducing the flaw size in any material, you increase the strength.

These springs provide a unique flexibility combined with a high temperature-resistance that metals would not be able to stand.

Flexible

Dimensions	**150mm x 10mm**
Key Features	**Good toughness**
	Can be used where high temperature and tension are required
	Extremely hard and durable
	Good chemical-resistance
	Dense
More	**www.ceram.com**
Typical Applications	**Zirconia is known for its toughness and fine finish which make it suitable for cutting edges and watches. Other applications include medical prostheses, and pump seals and valves. The toughened form is used where these applications require extra toughness and flexibility. It is also used for ceramic kitchen knives.**

High-temperature spring
Manufacturer: Ceram

014

Reactive ceramics

This is a ceramic that likes to show off. When it is struck or provoked, it will react. Discovered in the 1880s by Pierre Curie, piezoelectric materials can best be described as materials that either generate a charge when deformed by hitting or bending, or change their dimension when an electric charge is applied to them.

As a sensing or transmitting element, there are many examples of piezoelectric devices in common use. The kitchen gas lighter, for example, uses them to generate a spark: a small crystal is struck which in turn generates energy in the form of a spark. A microphone works the same way, with air pressure deforming the crystals and converting the energy to a voltage, which is used to transmit sound.

Sports products are always good showcases for advanced materials. The Head ChipSystem™ tennis rackets use the reactive piezoelectric technology to produce a smart racket. At the heart of the technology are three parts: piezo reactive fibers, a circuit, and a microchip. Combined, this trio takes the impact energy of the ball hitting the racket and transfers it into an opposite force, thus reducing vibration.

Intelligence X Technology
tennis racket with
ChipSystem™
Manufacturer: Head

Dimensions	Racket head: 760mm²
Key Features	Motion sensitive
	Converts waste energy
	Energy-absorbing
	Increased stiffness
	Less fibration
More	www.advancedcerametrics.com
	www.head.com
	www.ceramtec.com
Typical Applications	Has uses in cigarette lighters, kitchen gas lighters, microphones, sound generating devices for sonar and ultrasound detectors, and tweeters in stereo speakers. The manufacturer ACI is currently looking into using the PZT technology to produce clothing and self-heating walking boots.

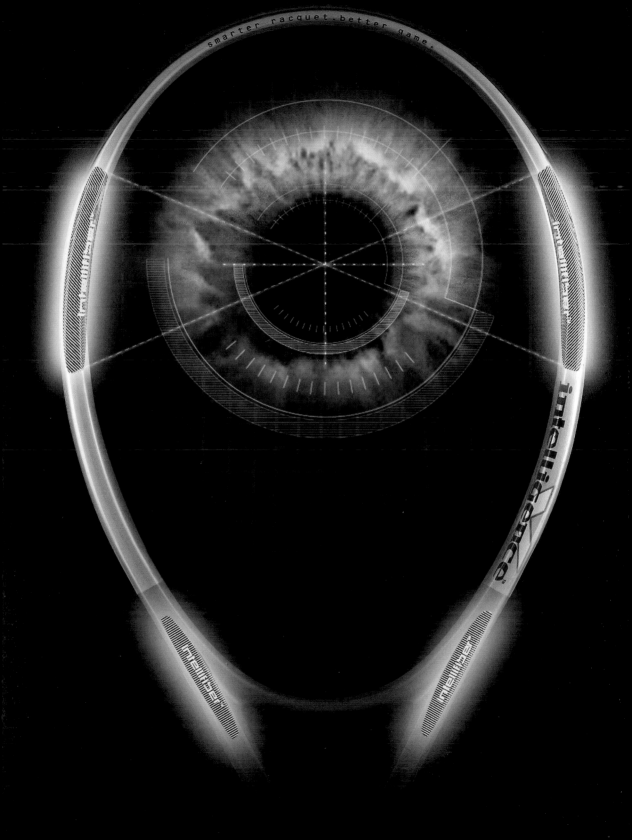

Diverse applications

This naturally occurring mineral is not strictly speaking a ceramic, but its physical properties mean that it is often put into this family. The uses of graphite are diverse. On a humble level, graphite makes an appearance in pencils, where its soft, slippery qualities are put to good use. But on a more ostentatious level, it is used for performance sports products. In these applications, it has an excellent strength-to-weight ratio, which, combined with energy-absorbing properties, makes it a contender in the market for high-spec sports gear, like tennis rackets and golf clubs.

Characterized by its silvery gray surface with a metallic sheen, these differing applications explain how this relatively soft, slippery form of carbon is marked by three main forms: flake graphite, made up of crystal structures; amorphous graphite, which is soft and non-crystalline; and synthetic graphite, which constitutes the largest commercially used form. Graphite's layered structure gives it that distinctive, slippery feel, which provides an excellent use as a lubricant especially in high temperatures.

The Status Graphite guitar
One-piece carbon graphite
monocoque molding with
compound arched top
Designer: Rob Green
Manufacturer: Status Graphite

Dimensions	990mm x 345mm; weight 2.75kg
Key Features	Energy-absorbing
	Good strength-to-weight ratio
	Low friction
	Nontoxic
	Good machinability
	Good resistance to chemicals
	Good electrical conductivity
	Stability and strength at high temperatures
	Excellent resistance to thermal shock
More	www.worldwidegraphite.com
	www.graphtekllc.com
	www.grafite.com
	www.advceramics.com
	www.ceramicindustry.com
	www.cevp.co.uk
	www.imerys.com
Typical Applications	Graphite is used in its various forms in a wide range of industries. The amorphous form is mixed with clay and used for pencil leads. It is used in various composite forms to reinforce plastics improving lightness, energy absorption, strength, and rigidity making it useful for performance sports goods like golf clubs, tennis rackets, and hockey sticks. Its ability to withstand extremes of temperature gives it applications in aerospace and transport.

018

Acoustic ceramics

Until relatively recently, most speakers have been shy to come out from behind the couch or from the corner of the room. But these speakers are part of a new generation, ambitious enough to decorate the ceiling.

The experimentation with new materials for speaker design is an ongoing process. This material crossover not only brings improved acoustic performance to the technology, but also brings new functional meanings that allow the product to live in a new context.

This story begins with Francesco Pellisari, an acoustic designer who, on a visit to Umbria, the heart of Italy's ceramics industry, caught sight of a discarded ceramic cone. Pellisari's tests found that the rigidity of ceramics could be applied to speakers: the rigidity enhances the frequency on the sounds. For the Seth range of speakers, the terracotta is fired at a high temperature and a glaze is applied. The platinum coat is applied on the third firing over the glaze.

These speakers are not just new materials in an old context: they extend the use of a new material, finding new decorative potential and new locations for the black box that sits in the corner of a room.

Key Features	Cost-effective
	Low density
	Fine, distinctive surface
	Can be formed with a variety of production methods
More	www.nacsound.it

Seth speaker in platinum-plated ceramic
Dimensions:
320mm x 140mm diameter
Designer: F. Pellisari
Manufacturer: NAC
Sound Srl, Italy

Atun speaker
Dimensions:
810mm high
Designers: Elizabeth
Frolet and F. Pellisari
Manufacturer: NAC
Sound Srl, Italy

Stays sharp

So why have a ceramic sharp edge in your kitchen? Why should you want to ditch those steel graters in favor of a high-tech ceramic material? There are several reasons why manufacturers will tell you ceramics are better, but the main reason lies in their characteristically hard-wearing quality, which means they will stay sharp for longer.

Within many areas of manufacturing, ceramics have taken the place of steel tools. For example, ceramic pressing for punching out aluminum drinks cans. This improves efficiency and cost effectiveness of production, allowing for tools to last 20 months without signs of wear, compared to two months for traditional metal tools.

Compared with traditional steel blades, ceramics are much harder. After time the edge of a forged metal blade, which is relatively soft in comparison, will "roll," lose its edge, and need to be sharpened. The harder ceramic blades will remain sharp for much longer. The chemical inertness of ceramic also means that it won't react with your food.

Kyocera ceramic grater
Manufacturer: Kyocera

Dimensions	89mm and 165mm diameter
Key Features	Hard-wearing
	Chemically inert
	Stays sharp
	Cost-effective production
More	www.kyocera.de
	www.kyoceratycom.com
	www.kyocera.co.jp
	www.sorma.net

Unlike earthenware, porcelain is a vitreous ceramic, which means it contains glass: this results in a product that can hold liquids. This product by designer KC Lo explores the material's potential for giftworthy products.

"I chose to use ceramics because they're cheap. It's the designer/maker thing, 'More bang for your buck,' like Inflate, who use easy to get hold of PVC with a cheap production process," says Lo. "It was also a challenge to produce giftware products as inexpensively as possible. Compared to doing an injection molding, which can be very expensive, the overall production process is cheap. You can stop after you have made a hundred if you need to. But if you were using injection molding you are committed to much larger orders.

More bang for your buck

Dimensions	70mm x 125mm x 35mm
Key Features	Good resistance to thermal shock
	Good hardness
	Distinctive white body
	Highly vitreous
	Watertight
More	Kc@netmatters.co.uk
	www.cpceramics.com

Albino Jigsaw oil lamp
Designer: KC Lo
Prototype: CP Ceramics
Manufacturer: First production run
by Norcroft China

"Albino Jigsaw is a simple tabletop oil lamp made out of white porcelain. Each piece of the jigsaw can hold 40ml of fuel. Its shape is formed like an individual piece of jigsaw, hence its name. Linking it with more pieces makes it like a giant jigsaw puzzle. When you're not using it, each piece of jigsaw can be stacked on top of each other to save valuable space and for easy storage.

"I wanted to make a tabletop object that would be fun and accessible. I didn't want to just improve on something. I mean, what else can you do. You can't just follow on and keep improving something, so where do you go next? So I thought, why not make it fun, give people a little something to smile about?"

Perforated containers
Dimensions:
120mm x 150mm diameter,
90mm x 250mm diameter
Designer: Stefanie Hering
Manufacturer: Hering Berlin

Hard and translucent

Most of us know porcelain as a distinctive material used for high-quality tableware. But this blend of clay, quartz, feldspar, and kaolin has uses and applications spread over a range of industries. Here it is used for its chemical and electrical properties rather than its aesthetic charm.

However, for its use in more domestic products, the hard nature of this highly vitrified ceramic has allowed designers to create objects that can have fine, thin wall sections and delicate detailing without the risk of the piece being easily broken, which might be the case with earthenware. Apart from the hardness its other distinctive feature, which is also common with bone china, is its elegant translucency.

The products of the Hering Berlin porcelain manufacturer are a body of work that tests these properties. The designs rely on the gentle forms and surface of this pale material. The products play with a subtle surface finish, patterns are created that alternate between matte and partly glazed surfaces, and fine changes of opaqueness and translucency. These are objects which play to the precious nature of the material, exploring the potential for its fine, paper-thin edges.

Stadium
Dimensions:
420mm x 240mm
Designer: Stefanie Hering
Manufacturer: Hering Berlin

Porcelain cups
Dimensions:
90mm x 80mm diameter
Designer: Stefanie Hering
Manufacturer: Hering Berlin

Key Features	**Translucent**
	Fine
	Very hard
	Chemically inert
More	**www.hering-berlin.de**

New applications

Porcelain is one of those materials loaded with a rich history associated with high-quality tableware and ornate figurines. Characterized by its whiteness, hardness, its ability to produce delicate forms, and its ghostly translucency, porcelain was first discovered around 600 AD in China. This is why it is often referred to as china or chinaware and it was not until the eighteenth century that Europeans were able to replicate it. Apart from being used for expensive dinner services, porcelain has also been one of the main ceramics used to produce electrical insulators and spark plugs.

In 1996, design group Droog were invited by Rosenthal, the well-known German porcelain manufacturer, to take part in an experimental project to find new applications and uses for this valued material. The result was a series of freethinking trials with this ancient material, which were not restricted to its familiar use as tableware. The group of products includes furniture, tableware, and lighting. The pieces include experimental production methods and new product typologies, and new combinations of ceramics with other materials.

Eggshell vase
Dimensions:
100mm x 100mm, 120mm x
120mm, 140mm x 140mm
Designer: Marcel Wanders
Manufacturer: Cappellini

Sponge Vase
Dimensions:
80mm x 120mm diameter
Designer: Marcel Wanders
Manufacturer: Cappellini

Key Features	**Good hardness**
	Good resistance to physical shock
	Translucent quality
	Distinctive white body
	Good abrasion- and wear-resistance
More	**www.rosenthal.de**
	www.droogdesign.nl
Typical Applications	**Commonly used in dental brackets and crowns, electrical insulators, tableware, and decorative figurines.**

Prototype porcelain stool
Dimensions:
500mm x 400mm x 250mm
Designer: Hella Jongerius
Manufacturer: Rosenthal

Thermal insulation

Siesta is a product with a foot firmly placed in the history of Spanish water carriers. Based on the traditional water carrier known as a botijo, this iconic shape has been updated, inspired by modern plastic water bottles.

Héctor Serrano explains: "We used white terracotta from the Alicante region in Valencia. This material has no added coloring or glaze, just a small portion of salt, which helps keep the water cool, even when the sun is hot. Depending on which region in Spain the terracotta comes from it will look different.

"The botijo was used by workers in Spain to carry water from their homes to the fields. The botijo keeps water cool in the heat of the sun. It has two holes, one for filling and one for drinking from. The larger hole can also be used to pour water into a pitcher or cup. The hole at the top is used to carry and hold the container.

"They were traditionally made by hand, using lathe production to make a small batch. It has since been sold to a manufacturer and is now slip-cast.

"Originally 30 pieces were made at a time. Now the design is being mass-produced and they make approximately 7,000 pieces a year."

Siesta
**Designers: Héctor Serrano,
Alberto Martinez, and
Ricky Martinez
Manufacturer: La Mediterranea**

Dimensions	360mm x 100mm diameter
Key Features	**Easily formed**
	Weather-resistant
	Good thermal protection
	Low temperature firing
	Low density
More	**www.la-mediterranea.es**
	www.hectorserrano.com
	hector@hectorserrano.com

Biscuity texture

Terracotta is one of the simplest expressions of ceramics. It is a clay with an unglazed, semi-fired body and, with its distinctive color and ability to withstand weathering, it is the choice for outdoor ceramics. The dry, dusty, biscuity texture of terracotta is obtained through washing the clay and mixing in fine particles of sand. Although the creamy red variety is the most common, it is also found in yellow and even a milky white.

The insulating properties of terracotta inspired this range of flowerpots by designer Martin Szekely. The form reflects the monastic nature of this simple material where the only decoration is the trace of the potter's fingers.

This project was part of a larger proposal by designers in the French Vallauris region near Nice. Since 1998, two designers have been invited each year to breathe new life into this indigenous material.

Dimensions	**490mm x 410mm diameter, 390mm x 315mm diameter, 300mm x 270mm diameter**
Key Features	**Cost-effective**
	Fine and distinctive surface
	Weather-resistant
	Can be formed by a range of production processes
	Low density
More	**www.kreo.com**
	www.martinszekely.com
Typical Applications	**Floor and roofing tiles, building bricks, and ornamental building parts.**

Vallauris flower bricks
Designer: Martin Szekely
Production: Lou Pignatier
Edition: Kreo

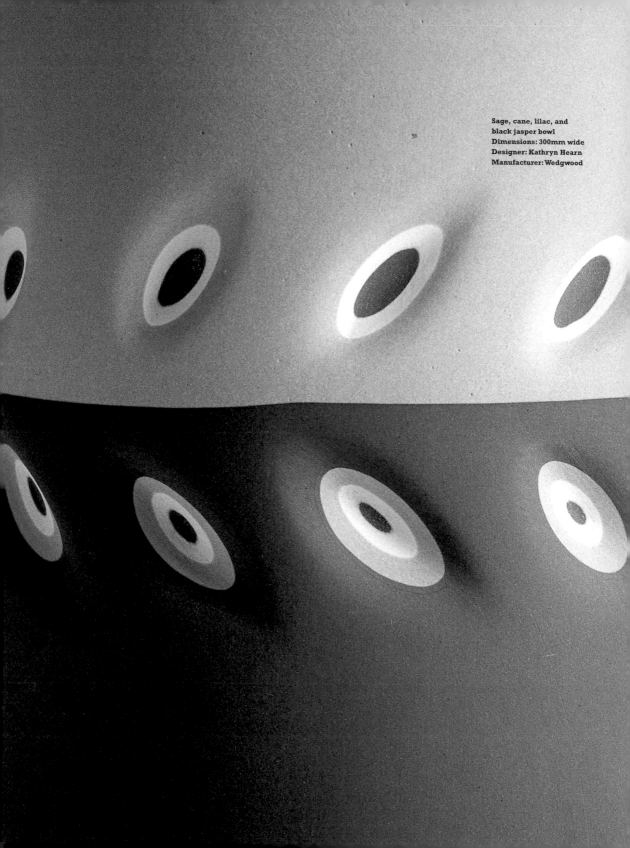

Sage, cane, lilac, and
black jasper bowl
Dimensions: 300mm wide
Designer: Kathryn Hearn
Manufacturer: Wedgwood

Strata-casting

Designer Kathryn Hearn has used Jasper stoneware to produce a range of pieces combining it with a unique production process, which explores new possibilities for this traditional Wedgwood ceramic. Through a process of slip-casting several layers, a strata of different colors is formed which are then exposed through various methods. This process is about opening up the ceramic surface to reveal a multilayered texture.

"I have made decorative pots and used molds of many types, even casting into sand, but usually I work with simple plaster molds where I can create surfaces that are intriguing and integral to the form. I make complex patterns which are achieved by putting striated inclusions into the mold before casting, also carving back the surface to reveal intimate landscapes," says Hearn.

The name stoneware does a good job of suggesting the qualities of this kind of material. Like porcelain and bone china, stoneware is a hard, water-resistant ceramic. The British tableware manufacturer Wedgwood uses it in a specific form known as Jasper, which is marked by its distinctive rough, stone-like textured finish.

Key Features	Not as easy to work as a clay but more stable in the firing
	Vitrified
	Fires at 2,161°F (1,183°C)
	Hard
	Opaque
	Stone-like quality
More	www.wedgwood.com
	k.hearn@csm.linst.ac.uk
Typical Applications	The hard and vitrified nature of stoneware means it has applications for water-resistant tableware without the need for glazing.

Small slipped vase with carved
recesses in Portland blue, pale blue,
and stone jasper
Dimensions: 250mm high
Designer: Kathryn Hearn
Manufacturer: Wedgwood

Loop Chair
Designer: Willy Guhl
Manufacturer: Eternit AG

Dimensions	545mm x 545mm x 765mm
Key Features	**Allows for thin wall sections to be constructed**
	Excellent chemical-resistance
	Scratch-resistant
	Will not support or maintain mold growth or fungi
	Lightweight
	Wide color range
	Scratch- and abrasion-resistant
	Life expectancy of at least 50 years
More	**www.eternit.co.uk**
	www.eternit.ch
	www.twentytwentyone.com
	www.wohnbedarf.ch
Typical Applications	**This product is mainly used in the building industry for external and internal wall cladding and roofing.**

Cement sheet

These smooth, organic forms contrast with the rough, imperfect, and gray cement from which they are formed. The reference to a building material is clear: take the properties of a construction material—strong, cheap, and weatherproof—and use them to create a new language for outdoor furniture.

A product of 1950s building technology, the concrete garden chair exploits the process of fiber cement, a process used to produce machine-made slabs for use in architecture. Originally reinforced using asbestos fiber, the material has since been replaced with cellulose fibers as a supporting substructure, which strengthens the material both in compression and tension.

Eternite is a patented sheet material used for walls and cladding. It is a mixture of cement and fiberglass, which allows for thin wall sections. The chair is produced as a sheet and folded around a mold.

The concrete chair is encountering a renaissance as a contemporary garden chair with the range being extended to include outdoor planters.

032

Shifting contexts

The traditional advantage ceramics offer over other materials such as wood and plastic, is its unique marriage with a glaze to provide a permanent bond and finish. The unique approach of this piece combines ceramics with an alternative traditional process.

Inspired by the ceramics collection housed in the Het Princessehof Museum in Leeuwarden, Holland, this Giant Prince vase forms part of a collection where the surface decoration takes on a new form. The pieces subvert the traditional glaze, which is applied to ceramics by introducing a method of ornamentation from another discipline. The embroidered porcelain vase creates a new approach to the surface design of this material where the combination of hard and soft materials creates a unique encounter between two materials and processes.

This piece continues the tradition of this internationally known designer, whose work is typified by experimenting with materials and shifting contexts to discover new possibilities for both old and new materials.

Dimensions	700mm x 850mm diameter
Key Features	Receptive to decorative glaze
	Elegant
More	www.jongeriuslab.com

Giant Prince porcelain vase
embroidered with cotton
Designer: Hella Jongerius
Client: Het Princessehof
Museum , Leeuwarden, Holland

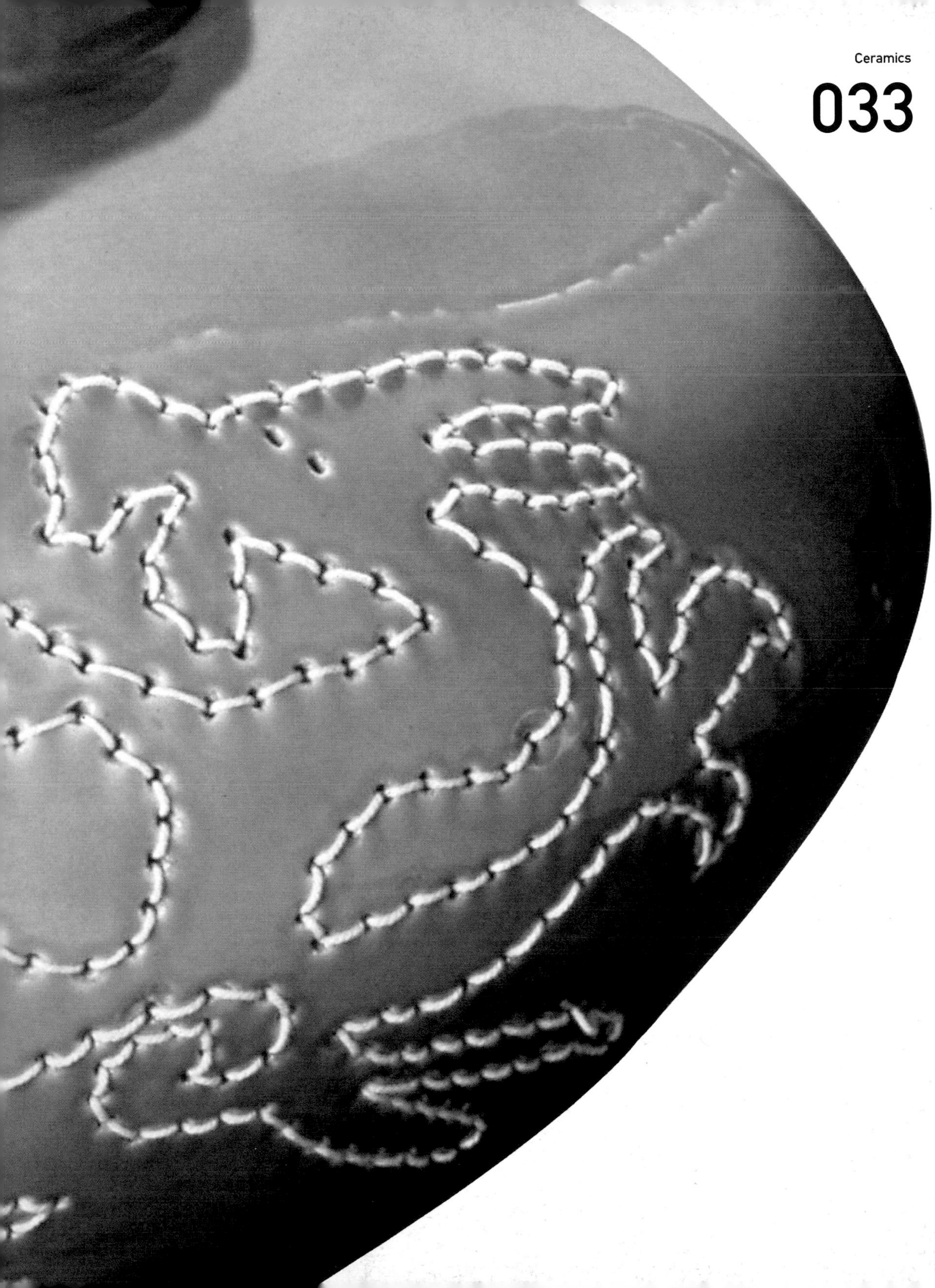

034

Porous and opaque

Polar Molar is a tabletop toothpick holder made in slip-cast, glazed earthernware by KC Lo.

"Inspiration for my design came from biological illustrations and models. It is designed so that the user can pick up toothpicks in the most hygenic way from the middle of the toothpick (not the ends). This is made possible because of the slot created in the middle of the block," says Lo.

"The name Polar describes its white, glazed body but also plays on the word poles, which also means sticks (in this case the toothpicks). And the word molar is used to symbolize teeth.

"One of the aims of Polar Molar is to allow the owner to put it on the dining table to spark-off interesting conversations among diners at the end of an otherwise boring dinner party!

"The channel requires that it is made in two pieces, which are stuck together to achieve the internal cavity."

Polar Molar Toothpick Holder
Designer: KC Lo
Prototype: CP Ceramics
Manufacturer: First production
run by Coral Ceramics

Dimensions	**32mm x 83mm x 100mm**
Key Features	**More prone to chipping than china**
	Less distortion during firing than china or porcelain
	Generally fired below 2,192°F (1,200°C)
	Cost-effective
More	**www.kclo.co.uk**
	www.cpceramics.com
Typical Applications	**Anything hollow such as teapots, vases, and figurines.**

Workhorse

With any industry, there are always materials which, through their balance of physical and chemical properties and cost, become widely used. They may not have any great distinguishing properties or anything extraordinary about them, but they offer the right balance of characteristics at the right price. In the area of advanced ceramics, alumina is this type of material, but in the area of traditional ceramics, earthenware is the workhorse. It is used in many ceramic products from small items of tableware to large pieces of sanitary ware.

Earthenware is a porous, opaque ceramic and, unlike the vitreous and translucent porcelain or china, needs to be glazed to be watertight and hold liquid. One of the common tests used to distinguish this material is to put your tongue on the unglazed underside of a piece to test its absorbency. Although it is not as strong or as dense as china or porcelain and is prone to chipping, it has the advantage of less distortion in lower firing temperatures and is thus more stable during processing.

Dimensions	110mm x 480mm diameter, 140mm x 610mm diameter
Key Features	Generally fired below 2,192°F (1,200°C)
	Less distortion during firing than porcelain or china
	Versatile range of processes available
	Cost-effective
	More prone to chipping than china
	Not as dense as stoneware
More	www.satyendra-pakhale.com
Typical Applications	Used in all product areas from large sanitary ware to mugs and plates.

Kalpa-Ceramic Vase and Bowl
in One Object
Designer: Satyendra Pakhalé

Porcelain Hemispheres in
concrete to be used as
architectural detail or furniture
Dimensions:
150mm x 150mm x 40mm
Designers: Victoria Rothschild
and Anna Usborne

How do you humanize the urban and rough image of concrete? That was the starting point for this project by Victoria Rothschild and Anna Usborne. While still students at the Royal College of Art in London, they produced this range of experiments for a competition sponsored by the British Cement Association. Using a mixture of different ceramic materials like terracotta, glass, and porcelain they have created an ensemble of ideas pushing the boundaries and cultural definition of concrete.

All the pieces were shaped and cut using a diamond saw. For the polishing and smoothing, a flatbed grinder was used. The cement used was either Snowcrete or White Ciment Fondu Secar 71, which is a refractory ceramic. The gray cement was Portland cement. The mix was three parts aggregate to one part cement.

Key Features	**Exceptional compression strength**
	Can be used for low- or high-volume production
	A range of aggregates can be used for a variety of effects
	Colors can be changed easily
	Fairly low-cost tooling
	High labor cost
More	**www.cementindustry.co.uk**
	www.concrete-info.com
Typical Applications	**The majority of concrete used is for building applications. However, through various artists and designers exploring new possibilities for the material, new applications have been discovered which include jewelry, furniture, kitchen work surfaces, and tableware.**

Gritty surface

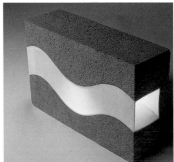

Decorative wall feature
Dimensions:
300mm x 200mm x 80mm
Designers: Victoria Rothschild
and Anna Usborne

Terracotta and concrete block
Dimensions:
300mm x 200mm x 80mm
Designers: Victoria Rothschild
and Anna Usborne

Porcelain wavy light strip
in concrete
Dimensions:
150mm x 100mm x 60mm
Designers: Victoria Rothschild
and Anna Usborne

038

Surprise surface

This is one of the superior types of cements.
Available in rich chocolate and dark gray
tones or even a highly polished white.
This cement offers the designer far more
potential than Portland cement to
experiment with the more decorative and
aesthetic qualities of this abundant material.

Compared to Portland cement, which is
based on silica and limestone, Ciment Fondu
has a range of advantages: it has the ability
to form far more complex shapes and to
withstand temperatures up to 3,632°F
(2,000°C) compared with 932°F (500°C)
for Portland cement; it is also much
more durable.

Kelvin J. Birk is a gold and silver designer
who enjoys exploring the unexpected
encounter between the precious and the
utility. The specific use of Ciment Fondu
provides the freedom to experiment with
a range of finishes and colorings.

Round Gilded Bowl
Designer: Kelvin J. Birk

Dimensions	300mm diameter
Key Features	**Ability to form complex shapes**
	Quick-drying but long working time
	Fast mold turnaround
	Achieves in 24 hours the strength that takes Portland cement 28 days
	Same working time
	Superior surface finish
	Good corrosion-resistance
More	**www.lcainc.com**
Typical Applications	**Quick-drying flooring where paint or polymer coverings need to be set over the top. It is also the basis for fast-set tile adhesive and floor-leveling compounds. Also as a medium for artists and craftsmen and high temperature applications in the steel industry.**

Dimensions	850mm x 720mm x 650mm
Key Features	No tooling
	Batch-production
	Requires high skill
More	www.satyendra-pakhale.com
Typical Applications	The process of throwing is used to make a whole range of products from tableware to art pieces and outdoor furniture.

Industrial shapes

Flower Offering ceramic chair
Designer: Satyendra Pakhalé
Manufacturer: Atelier Satyendra Pakhalé

Apart from bathroom sanitary ware, examples of ceramics used for furniture are fairly limited. However, the highly distinctive forms produced by designer Satyendra Pakhalé bring a unique visual language to this area of design.

The references to mass-produced industrial shapes are combined with the ancient process of turning clay on a wheel to produce a range of large-scale furniture pieces.

"The choice of clay was critical in deciding which clay mixture would be elastic enough to throw while keeping the desired strength. Equal drying of the different wall thickness of the thrown clay parts and firing it without cracks was a challenge," says Pakhalé.

The time it takes a piece to dry before firing is related to several criteria, the clay body (mixture), its scale, complexity and, thickness. A consistent drying time is essential and for this complex piece it took two to three weeks. Initially, there were problems of cracking when the chair was fired as a complete piece, the design had to be adapted resulting in the front and back parts being produced separately. These were joined together after firing with a two-part polyurethane glue.

Initially produced using a craft process, the chair has since been developed to take advantage of industrial production. It is now produced using pressure-cast molds similar to those used in the sanitary ware industry.

Digital tableware

Making prototypes used to mean employing a model maker to make your design by hand. Today many industries are exploiting the various forms of rapid prototyping to produce these models. These CAD-driven machines provide designers with the ability to produce samples and prototypes faster and more cost effectively than traditional methods.

Some of the most common involve polymer resins. However, some manufacturers believe that plaster can give a much better representation of a final ceramic design than these resins, with a look and feel more akin to a biscuit-fired ceramic. Manufacturers like Royal Doulton use a three axis milling machine driven by a CAD program to carve out wet plaster.

Initially a block of plaster is cast which is allowed to dry for about 30 minutes. At this stage, the plaster is hard but still wet and is ready to be cut. By cutting the plaster in this wet state the amount of dry dust that would be produced if it were dry is greatly reduced. This means that apart from creating a cleaner working environment, the wearing on the tool is also reduced.

The advantage of CAD-driven models is not restricted to faster turnaround times for mock-ups; the use of computer modeling allows for a far greater range of complex surface patterns to be created, which otherwise would have been difficult using traditional methods.

Key Features	Fast turnaround of samples
	Allows for fine and complicated detailing
	Expands scope for design
	The fast turnaround allows for more concepts to be considered
	The plaster more closely resembles the final material than a resin version
More	www.royaldoulton.com
	www.the-hothouse.com
Typical Applications	This process can be used on any product or shape, which can be generated by computer. The only size restriction is that of the machine, but otherwise any type of product can be prototyped.

Touch range
Manufacturer: Royal Doulton

Line drawing

From slots and holes to complicated patterns and shapes, and from drilling to scribing, flat sheets of ceramics can be cut to any shape you can draw with a pencil. Laser-cutting is a well-known process for cutting intricate shapes from flat materials. Used for cutting wood, metal, and glass, it offers designers the opportunity to create decoration or intricate individual components from a flat sheet.

But the chance to create complex patterns in ceramic is not as widely exploited or as well known as it is for other materials. The process offers flexibility in terms of production, speed, and opportunity to create details with very high tolerances. Starting from a CAD file and with no tooling, the process is cost-effective for one-offs or batch production. But the really interesting thing with this process is that it creates components that have a totally different quality to other materials. These samples of laser-cut alumina are reminiscent of rigid, brittle pieces of stiff, cold paper. With a scratchy, almost chalky surface and a soft translucency, they suggest applications which are not just for electronics.

Dimensions	100 microns–2mm
	Tile sizes vary depending on thickness and availability
Key Features	Can be cut directly from a CAD file
	No tooling
	Flexible production process
	Suitable for low- or high-production volumes
	Tolerance can be controlled to 20 microns
	Can be used for a variety of materials
More	www.lasercutting.co.uk
Typical Applications	Due to the cost of the ceramic substrate, laser-cut ceramics are generally used on a small scale with applications in the microelectronic industry as a basis for printed circuitry.

Range of laser-cut samples
produced from alumina substrates
Manufacturer: Laser Cutting UK

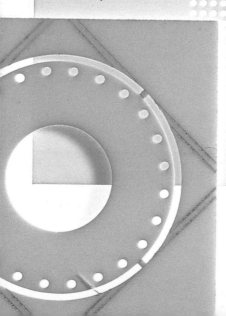

Cost-efficient

So you've designed that new ashtray or the toothpick holder for a client who owns a chain of bars and restaurants who has decided he needs 500 units rather than the 5,000 originally ordered. What do you do? You need to find another supplier because the agent who represents the manufacturers won't return your call for less than 2,500 units.

There are many companies whose business is to take up orders from designers dealing in niche products based on medium-scale production runs. Due to its abundant source of good clay and coal, Stoke-on-Trent is the center of ceramic production in the UK. The area is a microcosm of the whole ceramics industry and is one of the major producers of ceramic products in the world. It offers a one-stop range of products for a whole list of packaging, promotional, domestic, and industrial products from ornamental and functional ceramics such as door handles, bathroom fittings and accessories, aromatherapy bowls, and exterior plaques to bespoke artifacts. Manufacturers in the area use just about every ceramic production process available including slip-casting solid or hollow, high-pressure casting used for bar ware, extruding, wet-pressing, ram-pressing, turning, and powder-pressing.

Dimensions	455mm x 60mm diameter
Key Features	Low- or high-volume production runs
	Can be used for a range of materials
	Can have low tooling costs
More	www.wades.co.uk
	www.johnson-tiles.com
	www.matthey.com
	www.churchillchina.com
Typical Applications	Turning is used to make symmetrical products and components including door handles, pestle handles, and electrical insulators.

Porcelain rolling pin with
beech wood handles
Manufacturer: Wade Ceramics

044

Viscous plastic processing (VPP) is a process for forming ceramics that have been purged of microstructural defects or flaws. This gives the material improved characteristics.

The toughness of ceramics is reduced by microscopic defects within the material. These tiny faults mean the material's ability to plastically deform is reduced. So if you put the material under tension, it is likely to break. By removing these small pockets of air, cracks, and amassing of ceramic lumps, all the ceramic's flaws are eliminated.

This means that the type of products, the types of production methods used, and a whole range of simple and complex shapes can be produced in a variety of materials, which would have been difficult or impossible before.

Conventional plastic-forming techniques can be used to form complex thin, flat sheet extrusions and moldings. The enhanced properties it offers ceramics allows for objects to be produced with thinner wall sections and reduced weight, without compromising on performance.

Conventional or novel plastic-forming processes may be used to shape the ceramic paste and the green material is easily machined, offering economies for difficult shapes. Viscous plastic processing can result in products of much greater flexural strength than those achieved by powder-pressing, for example.

Dependent upon the grain size of the powder, a superior surface finish is obtained. VPP provides further advantages by improving other flaw-controlled properties such as translucency, electrical resistivity, and dielectric loss.

Dimensions	10mm diameter
Key Features	**Allows for products of a greater flexural strength**
	Can be processed using a large variety of techniques
	Offers reduced weight
	Allows for thinner wall sections
	Improved creep-resistance
	Increased fracture toughness
	Consistency in strength from component to component
	Uses standard bodies
	Binders are commodity nonhazardous chemicals
	Water-based binder solution
	Low binder levels compared to competing injection molding systems
	Rapid production
More	**www.ceram.com**
Typical Applications	**Plastic-forming techniques can be used to form complex shapes, thin sheets, or extrusions. Their ability to create thin wall sections without compromising on strength means they can be used where component reliability is essential. On a more general level, it can be used in anything from tableware to engineering applications.**

Flawless

Knot
Manufacturer: Ceram

Compressive strength

By brick clay I mean the reddish, dusty, gritty, and sand-rough material that is the most ancient of artificial building materials. There are thousands of alternative shapes and functions in which they are available and they give the most widely used example of the compression strength of ceramics.

There are two widely used types of brick clays, which manifest themselves in two colors: the first consists of non-chalky clays, sand feldspar minerals, and iron compounds which, after firing, become salmon colored; the second comprises a more limey clay which contains 40 percent calcium carbonate, that are yellow when fired. However, the precise type and color of clay is dependent on the area they are dug from, the method of firing, and the type of kiln used.

There are many companies who mass-produce standard bricks in an assortment of standard shapes and sizes. The distinguishing feature of H.G. Matthews is their ability to produce individual and specific architectural building products. Their handmade bricks are considered to be some of the finest bricks available, their quality based on appearance, character, and range of colors, including orange, browns, and light and dark purples. With a large percentage of their bricks handmade, they offer a flexible production base from one-offs to mass-production.

Sample of brick clay
Manufacturer: H.G. Matthews

Key Features	**Excellent uniformity of strength**
	Excellent crushing strength
	Distinctive surface
	Can be formed with a range of processes
	Weather-resistant
More	**www.hgmatthews.com**
	www.ibstock.co.uk
	www.imerys-structure.com
	www.yorkhandmade.co.uk
Typical Applications	**Walls, paving, date bricks, friezes, plinths, bricks, and architectural special moldings.**

One of the major industries in which ceramics are used widely is within refractory applications. Their unique heat- and flame-resistance puts them on top of the material tree when it comes to these thermal properties. However, these are products which take on a different form to the solid brick variety and allow for this heat advantage to be used in a range of applications outside of the industrial ovens.

This product provides the opportunity for flexibility in a flame barrier. There are many applications where fire safety is an issue, ranging from aerospace, outerspace, and automotive to industrial.

These fibers are continuous and strong which means they can be used without the need for additional support. They can be made into a range of products including paper, yarns, fabrics, tapes, and sewing thread and also in a range of grades for both non-structural and load-bearing applications. Considering this material is used to deflect heat from jet engines, you know this is serious stuff.

Flexible flame barrier

Dimensions	910mm–1,470mm wide. Special order items are available to meet the needs of the application
Key Features	High temperature applications up to 2,500°F (1,371°C)
	Flexible
	Good resistance to abrasion
	Low elongation at operating temperatures
	Low shrinkage at operating temperatures
	Good chemical-resistance
	Low thermal conductivity
	Thermal shock resistance
	Low porosity
More	www.mmm.com/ceramics
Typical Applications	One of the big markets for these materials is in the area of fire safety, including suits for racing car drivers, soft panels for the cockpits of Formula 1 cars, floor mats for cockpits, industrial applications for furnace curtains, structural reinforcement, sewn refractory parts and shapes, fire barriers, and insulation shields.

Nextel™ ceramic textiles
Manufacturer: 3M™

Micro ceramics

Materials serve as many discreet functions in their own rights as they do for the objects which they form. Like ingredients added to food recipes, they perform particular functions designed to enhance the performance of their host. Available in a range of microscopic sizes, this application for ceramic spheres has offered a wide range of industries increased performance.

3M™ produce two groups of ceramic spheres: Z-Light Spheres™ and Zeeospheres™. Without a microscope, these spheres appear as a fine powder and are used to fulfill a wide range of applications in different industries. These semi-transparent, white colored, fine particles can offer increased hardness and abrasion-resistance when mixed in to a variety of coatings. The chemical inertness of ceramics is also an excellent feature for providing an inert protective barrier within a paint or coating, offering protection from various types of chemicals, weathering, and corrosion. The spherical shape also helps material flow for plastic-molding applications.

Depending on what an application requires, these strong, hard, inert, and hollow spheres offer the designer the opportunity to increase the performance of a range of products or materials.

Dimensions	Three white grades: 12, 23–25, and 42–45 microns
Key Features	Good hardness
	Excellent abrasion-resistance
	Chemically inert
	Low density
	Available in a range of particle sizes
More	www.3m.com
Typical Applications	The various features of ceramics offer benefits for a range of applications. Their hollow form can be used to help create a thermal barrier in various materials. Their hardness is used to increase wear-resistance of components or surfaces. Their chemical inertness can be used when they are mixed with coatings to help improve chemical-resistance.

W610 Zeeospheres™
Manufacturer: 3M

Magnetic

Ceramic magnets, more commonly referred to as Ferrite magnets, are used in everything from fridge magnets to toys. They are nothing to look at—black, dirty, and cheap. Their low cost goes some way to explaining why they are so popular, combined with properties which make them suitable for a range of environments and applications. Although magnets can be injection molded, they are generally made by die-pressing powder made up of 80 percent iron oxide and 20 percent barium or strontium oxide. The molded components are then sintered at approximately 2,192°F (1,200°C).

With these magnets available in an assortment of forms, like strips and tapes, they offer many potential applications. And who would have thought you could buy ceramics on rolls and cut them with a pair of scissors. Magnets are fun!

Key Features	Cost-effective
	Excellent resistance to demagnetization
	Can be magnetized before or after assembly
	Operating temperatures of between −40°F (−40°C) to +482°F (+250°C)
	Good chemical-resistance
	Good hardness
	Good resistance to corrosion
More	www.magnetapplications.com
Typical Applications	Sintered ferrite or ceramic magnets are used in a variety of industrial and commercial applications. They can be formed into a range of products including blocks, rings, discs, tapes, and flexible strips.

Molded ceramic magnets
Manufacturer:
Magnet Applications

Key Features	**Can be machined and cut using ordinary metal working tools**
	Withstands high temperatures, up to 1,832°F (1,000°C)
	No firing required after machining
	Nonporous and nonshrinking
More	**www.corning.com**
	www.precision-ceramics.co.uk
Typical Applications	**Electrical and thermal insulators, structural components, and electrical equipment.**

No tooling

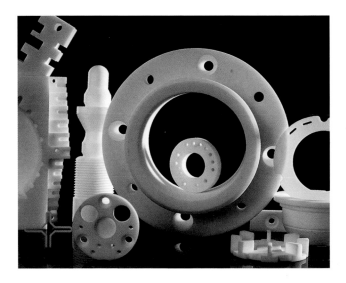

Macor® components
Manufacturer:
Precision Ceramics

So you've made that visual model, the stereo lithography sample looks great, but now you need to have the component tested in the right material. Ceramics can be the most immediate of materials, in the sense that you can manipulate a piece of clay with your hands. But then it needs to be fired, maybe glazed, and it will also shrink once you have taken it from the kiln, which can sometimes make things awkward. Here you have a material with the benefits of ceramics combined with some of the machinable qualities of metals.

Macor is a strong, rigid material, which is pure white and can be polished. By drilling, grinding, turning, sawing, polishing, and milling, it has processing qualities closer to metal than ceramic. The advantage of this strong, rigid material is that it is a ceramic which can be exploited by all of the above, which means there is no expensive tooling, contraction, or movement during firing and no frustrating delays. It is a material that is ideal for getting samples of prototypes or even low quantities of a ceramic component with less of the processing in between, which ultimately reduces development time and the cost of fabrication.

054

Electronic ceramics

Imagine conductive cups and saucers and other everyday banal objects that can talk to each other; a world where plates can talk to other electronic products in the kitchen, where conductive electronic circuits can be applied to ceramic objects.

Thick-film metallizing offers the potential for the physical properties of two materials to be joined together for a common interest. This is a network of conductive tracks, resistors, and capacitors placed over a ceramic substrate used for applications where standard fiberglass PCBs just won't do. It is a process for screen-printing precious metals like silver, gold, and platinum onto ceramic substrates. Apart from the advantages offered over conventional fiberglass PCBs, these ceramic circuits have a much higher operating temperature. They also differ in that they add material rather than etching it away.

The process involves screen-printing layers of the metals onto what is usually alumina or aluminum nitride, which is then fired to make a permanent physical bond. Subsequent layers can be added to form separate circuits. These are sandwiched between nonconductive barriers that allow for a complex grid of circuits that can function independently or together.

This is an industrial process that invites designers to explore the crossover of ceramics and electronics.

Key Features	**Higher operating temperature than conventional PCBs**
	High adhesion strength
	Custom-designed electronic circuit
	Can be printed single- or double-sided
	Insulation
	Excellent mechanical properties
	High level of accuracy
	Plated-through holes, unusual shapes, different thicknesses
More	**www.ceramtec.de**
	www.coorstek.com
	www.ukgeneralhybrid.com
	www.hlt.co.uk
Typical Applications	**Products range from custom-designed thick-film hybrids and surface-mount assemblies to standard products such as high voltage, high-value resistors; specialized resistor networks; and chip resistors. Applications are diverse, ranging from consumer through to military requirements.**

Electronic ceramic component parts Manufacturer: UK General Hybrid

057 Glass

Color-sequencing

Amy Cushing's fused glass pieces rely on a highly scientific recipe to create a unique range of color combinations and color-changing pieces. Cushing's company Mosquito™ combines this very controlled working method with a personal aesthetic that embraces materials and color.

Melting and blending glass is one of the oldest forms of natural glass production. Cushing begins by working cold with a palette of 20 colors. Threads, rods, and strips are layered over a clear sheet of glass, which is then fired and reworked by cutting, finishing, and firing again, up to four times. From the original 20 colors endless color combinations are produced. But the real skill lies in methodical experimentation, which gives a certain degree of predictability. Each piece of glass has to have the same expansion rate to avoid cracking in the kiln, and color change and temperature is noted. Cushing's blended experiments demonstrate the full potential for fused colored glass.

Dimensions	**200mm x 200mm**
	Maximum size for single piece: 500mm x 500mm
Key Features	**Allows for detail in small pieces**
	Can also cover large areas
	Infinite variety of color
	Low tooling costs
	Production volumes limited by handmade process
More	**www.nationalglasscentre.com**
Typical Applications	**Has uses for wall tiles, tableware, platters, dishes, partition walls, hanging installations, and jewelry.**

Detail from fused wall piece
Designer: Amy Cushing
with Ella Doran

Cat friendly

Dimensions	100mm x 160mm x 90mm
Key Features	Long cooling process compared to other methods
	Well suited to thick walled products
More	www.harrikoskinen.com

Glass takes on a thick, syrup-like form when heated. As it cools it takes on the exact form and surface detail of its mold. This simple practice is one of the oldest glass production methods that dates back to the ancient Egyptians, if not further. The Block Lamp, a thick, heavy, solid form, with a sandblasted internal shape, makes a direct reference to this ancient technique.

The idea for the Block Lamp, which is made from standard soda-lime glass, was conceived by Harri Koskinen during a sponsored college project at the University of Art and Design in Helsinki, Finland.

He examined cast glass as a specific production process and economized by using one graphite mold to create two identical parts. The original design was easily reproduced in a small batch of 50 units. When the rights were acquired by the Swedish producer, Design House, production naturally increased and the lamp has since been mass-produced. A maximum wattage of 25W is recommended so that the lamp does not get hot, but just warm enough for cats to fight over who gets to sit on it, which, according to Koskinen, is a common problem if you have more than one cat!

Block Lamp
Designer: Harri Koskinen
Manufacturer: Design
House, Stockholm

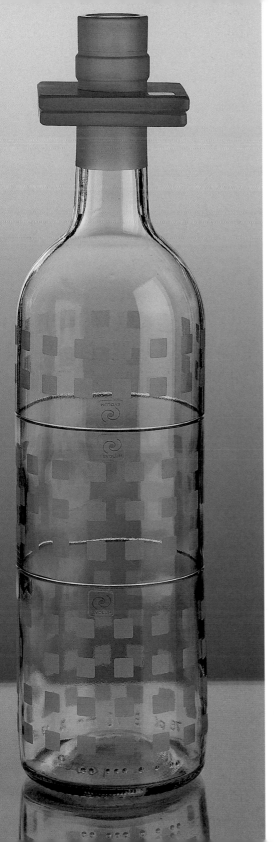

The Double Life of a Wine Bottle
from the Evolum Range
Designer: Jukka Isotalo

Glass

061

Reuse

Started as a project in 1989 as a result of
the "economical and ecological crisis," Jukka
Isotalo's bottles explore the possibility of
cold-working glassware by the economical
recycling of found bottles to create original
products with new functions.

"I started to make these products in 1989
while I was studying as an exchange student
at the University College of Arts, Crafts, and
Design in Stockholm, Sweden. I didn't have
enough money to travel to Finland for
Christmas and I was quite fed up with the
material overload the world was, and is,
suffering. I noticed all the bottles we had in
our studio in the glass department. I decided
to tackle the economical and ecological crisis
at the same time and made some vases out
of bottles for the Christmas fair. They were
a big success," explains Isotalo.

All of Isotalo's products are handmade from
nonrefillable bottles and surplus glass from
glaziers' shops. Sandblasting provides
decoration and no acid-etching is used. This
range is an example of how creative solutions
can arise from the most restrictive situations.

Dimensions	300mm x 100mm
Key Features	Low tooling but labor-intensive
	Ecological use of material
	Ecological production
More	jukka.isotalo@evolum.fi;
	Tel: +358 (0)9 8240 3000
	Pengerkatu 29, 00500 Helsinki, Finland
Typical Applications	Decoration and storage.

Textured water

Contained in every piece of glass is the latent ability to take on a new identity. Smooth, sleek, and flat polished glass can be contorted into heavy, delicious textures. To provoke this transformation, heat and a mold are needed.

Kiln-cast is a process of forming float glass over refractory molds to create textures and patterns on the surface of a piece of glass. With the range of surface effects that can be created, kiln-cast glass is becoming an increasingly common material within contemporary architecture and interior design.

Standard float glass is laid over ceramic, sand, plaster, or concrete molds depending on the desired texture and effect. When heated the glass relaxes over the molds to pick up the forms and texture. It is then slowly cooled and annealed. This can take anything from 12 hours to a week depending on its thickness and size.

As with any production process that uses molds, prices reduce according to the number of final units. Casting produces sheets with a depth of approximately 100mm which can then have a range of colors and finishes applied such as mirroring or sandblasting.

Cast glass not only allows for new visual organic, rhythmic, and geometric possibilities, but also provides a great tactile surface that makes you just want to touch it.

Dimensions	**Available up to a maximum size of 3,150mm x 1,750mm in 4mm–25mm thickness in float glass**
Key Features	**Endless possibilities for decoration**
	Can be bent or curved
	Can be one-off or batch-produced
	Low tooling costs for one-off pieces
	Handmade process
	Cost-effective compared with other decorative materials
	Good range of possibilities for coatings
	Can be toughened or laminated to British Standard 6206
More	**www.fusionglass.co.uk**
Typical Applications	**Partitions, doors, screens, commissioned features, flooring, signage-cladding, balustrades, counters, lighting, furniture, and sculpture.**

Kiln-cast glass
Designer: Fusion Glass Designs Ltd.

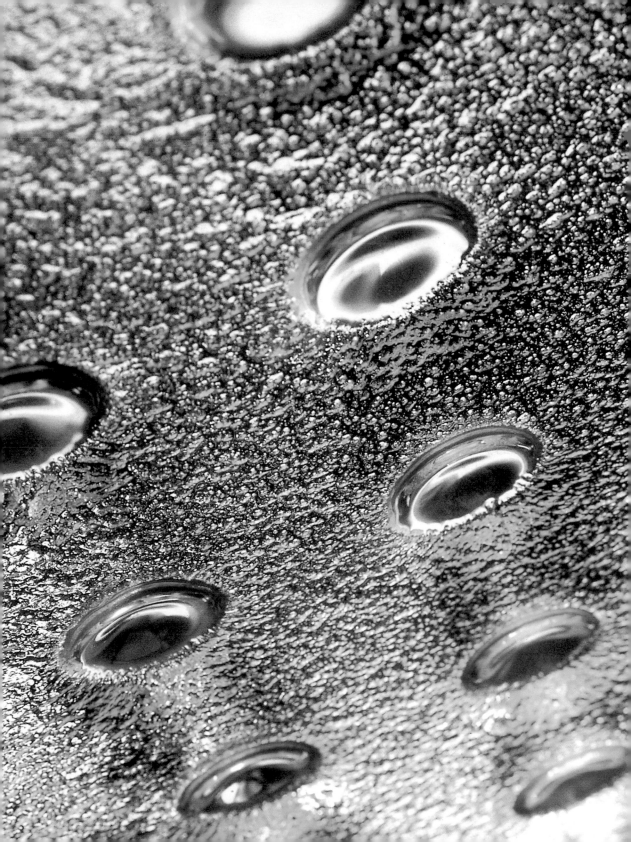

3D-frosting

Perfect for decorating any type of flat or formed glass, sandblasting is also an economic way of creating a surface effect for one-off or batch-produced products. This process is not limited to flat patterns but can also be used to create deep recesses and cut holes. Colors can be introduced by adding a pigment.

To achieve this permanently frosted effect, tiny particles of grit and air are sprayed on to the surface resulting in fine scratches. Elaborate patterns can be created using a stencil, and in the hands of a skilled craftsman, sandblasting can create delicately shaded areas. The introduction of a clear coating to protect the surface has meant that greasy fingerprints which would normally be left on a sandblasted surface are no longer a problem—making it a viable alternative to acid-etching but with less subtle detailing.

Dimensions	**Maximum sheet width: 2,286mm or, as Glacien Glass suggest, "any size as long it fits through the door"**
	Maximum recommended depth for deep sandblasting: approximately 5mm
Key Features	**Excellent potential for surface decoration**
	Can be applied to flat or formed glass
	Flexible working process
More	**www.glacienglass.co.uk**
	www.glass-design.com
	www.taylorsglass.co.uk
	www.glassco.co.uk
	www.pilkington.com
Typical Applications	**Doors, shower screens, furniture, tableware, and protective barriers.**

The clear glass marbles with twisting swirls of color embedded in them are the result of a simple process which can produce 14–16 million unique pieces per day.

To mass-produce marbles, molten glass is extruded into square or round canes. These lengths are then snipped into small, regular-sized pieces which are dropped on to a series of interlocking, threaded rollers. As they pass down the length of the rollers they are gradually rounded off into spheres and simultaneously cooled. The spiral pattern in clear marbles results from colored glass being blended with the rods before being sheared off into small pieces. The internal swirling shapes result from the canes constantly turning over on the rollers.

Marbles are one of the oldest toys known, and date back to the ancient Egyptians who buried them in tombs for use in the afterlife. They are also mentioned in ancient Greek literature. The earliest marbles were made of clay, wood, stone, and other hard materials. Glass marbles were not introduced until the mid-twentieth century. Today there is a healthy collectors' market of both machine and handmade marbles all over the world.

Hard and unique

Key Features	High volume production
	Every piece is unique
	Very cheap unit costs
	Durable
More	www.megamarbles.com
	Teign Valley Glass, Newton Abbot, Devon, UK Tel: +44 (0)1626 835358

Murano glass bowl
Designer: Unknown
Manufacturer: Murano Glass

These multicolored bowls are the result of a process that is over a thousand years old, the Millefiori "1,000 Flowers" technique, whereby objects are produced using thinly sliced multicolored sections of glass.

To make a Millefiori bowl you will need:
A kiln or glass-melting furnace
Flat ceramic plates (for fusing)
Dome-shaped ceramic form for slumping
Pincers and shears
A long-handled tool for transporting the plates and forms in and out of the furnace

• First, make the rods. Preheat your kiln. Heat some glass and stretch it out into strips—do this with a number of colors.
• Roll the strips together into a roll shape about 50mm in diameter. To achieve the thinness of the final rods (some are just 1mm) you will need to stretch the roll at both ends, this will depend on the size of your bowl. This should all be done while the glass is still hot.
• Once you have made your rods, allow them to cool enough to be picked up. Cut these rods into short lengths (about 5mm) and arrange them into a disc on your ceramic plates and reheat long enough for the pieces to become soft. Press the pieces flat and squash them together to remove any gaps and reheat until they have fused together and the glass pieces can be picked as a single sheet.
• To form the bowl place the soft sheet over your ceramic mold and place in the kiln until it softens enough to form a smooth shape over the mold. Take the mold out and remove the glass bowl. Once the glass has cooled you can grind and polish if you wish.

Dimensions	130mm x 80mm
Key Features	Unique decorative outcome
	Low tooling costs
	Low- to medium-scale production volumes
	Small alterations can be made to each item
More	www.langfords.com
	www.doge.it/murano/muranoi.htm
Typical Applications	Tableware and ornaments.

Fused mosaics

068

Patterned surface

Pressed glassware was first used in the early nineteenth century in the US to produce furniture handles and quickly became one of the most important production innovations since the introduction of glassblowing. One of its main advantages over blowing is its ability to produce fine detail on both the inside and outside of an object.

The basic process involves a lump of glass being squashed between an inner and outer mold. The thickness between these two parts controls the thickness of the final

glass piece. The inner and outer mold allows for this control and definition to be achieved on both surfaces. Its main disadvantage over blown glass products is that closed container shapes cannot be produced. The only requirement of any pressed shape is that the opening has a greater width than the base.

This process tends to produce robust, thick walled products. The dimples and points in this common lemon squeezer perfectly illustrate the pressed glass technique.

Lemon squeezer

Dimensions	**67mm x 127mm**
Key Features	**Automatic, semi-automatic, and manual process**
	Allows for detail on both sides of the glass
	Generally more expensive tooling than blown glass
	Allows for surface detailing that might otherwise not be possible without a secondary process
	Allows for a range of shapes
More	**www.nazeing-glass.com**
Typical Applications	**Lenses, exterior light fittings, street and display lighting, laboratory glass, ashtrays, and wall blocks.**

Glass eyes

Although there is strong competition from acrylic, glass still features prominently in optical prosthetics. The history of replacement eyes can be dated back to the ancient Egyptians and Romans who wore eyes made of painted clay attached to the outside of the socket with cloth.
The Egyptians also replaced the eyes of the dead. The Venetians made artificial glass eyes in the sixteenth century.

Modern day optical prosthetics can be traced back to 1832 when Ludwig Muller-Uri produced the first real glass eye in Germany. Today, eyes are made from cryolite—a special glass used specifically for glass eyes with little application in any other area.

To fit a prosthetic, the eye must be sized to the individual. The eyes are made by first lamp-working a tube of glass into a ball that has a nipple with which to hold and rotate the glass. Next, the ball is heated and worked down into a flatter, longer shape on to which the blood vessels are placed. The top of the ball around the iris is then blown up slightly to resemble a small mushroom shape. Then the sides of the ball are heated and gently sucked in to give the exact measurements and shape of the finished eye.

There are two types of glass eye—one is a hollow half-formed eye and the other is a thin bowl shape. Their use is dependent on the condition of the socket. These extraordinarily realistic looking eyes offer a very close match to the coloring, depth, and surface that you would expect from a real eye. They are testament to the craftsmanship involved in fitting and replicating these uniquely individual body parts.

Key Features	Biologically inert
	Neutral appearance
	Good scratch-resistance
	Hydroscopic, retains natural eye fluids, unlike plastic
More	www.ocularist.org
	www.kunstauge.ch
	www.augenprothetik-lauscha.de

Prosthetic eye
Designer: Rainer Spehl
Client: Worldwide

070

No longer just a part of seedy window displays, neon tubes are being taken into new territories. These intriguing, intestinal objects are created from a specific production process and materials to produce a unique language of form.

The continuous line of these structures is made by lamp-working a variety of colored glass canes with a wall thickness of about 1.2mm in lengths of about 1.5m. Once the shapes have been formed, electrodes are attached to either end of the loop. The piece is then placed in a vacuum where impurities are burnt out and a combination of neon, argon, and mercury gases are added. Once the object is complete, the ends with the electrodes are slotted into the base where the transformer is located.

Some of the most interesting objects feature a special Plasma Neon technology which creates a mesmerizing, moving cloud of gas in the tube—making the colors change according to the ambient temperature of a room. These techniques allow for specific forms to be handmade by just about anyone who wants to find an application or just plain likes them as they are.

New potential

Dimensions	500mm–2,500mm tall
Key Features	Highly distinctive
	Can be made to any design
	Low tooling and set up costs
	Can be incorporated into logos and artwork
Typical Applications	Can be used in lighting, interior decoration, signage, and in sculptural forms for interiors and exteriors.

People Sculptures
Designer: Rocco Borghese

Key Features	Low tooling investment
	Unit costs are high due to high labor costs
	Flexible production process
	Glass can be reused or recycled
	Soda-lime is one of the softer types of glass
More	marco.ss@clix.pt
Typical Applications	Suitable for drinking glasses, vases, bowls, and decorative pieces.

Portuguese design group, Proto, continually bring a range of projects that deal with specific materials and ideas to the international design arena. As with many of their ranges, these products require low investment in tooling because, as they state, "we are investing in creativity not complexity."

These handblown soda-lime tableware pieces—the Sweet Revolution range—were made in one of Portugal's oldest glass factories, the Marina Grande, which has been producing glass for about 250 years. The name Marina Grande is taken from the region where the factory is based, which is also known for its social and political activities. The glassblowers of the Marina Grande factory were an anarchic group pushing for social change. The name of this collection pays homage to these glassblowers and refers to the changes that occurred in Portugal in 1974 when the country was freed from dictatorship.

These pieces are handblown into wooden molds. With this level of production the glassblower can easily change and adapt the shapes, the thickness of the glass, and the internal shape of the containers. Production quantities vary from one-off pieces with wooden molds to several hundred or even thousands with alternative materials.

Sweet revolution

Water Carafe (1)
Dimensions:
190mm x 190mm x 220mm
Designer: Jose Viana
Client: Proto Design

Wine Decanter
Dimensions:
160mm x 160mm x 250mm
Designer: Marco Sousa
Santos
Client: Proto Design

Water Carafe (2)
Dimensions:
70mm x 70mm x 290mm
Designer: Paulo Parra
Client: Proto Design

These glass pieces say a lot about the manufacturing process of blown glass. The visual qualities of the material take a back seat in comparison to the production process.

The process of blowing glass into a hollow mold is the same for batch-produced studio glass as it is for mass-produced high volume glass. However, there are many technical restrictions placed upon this technique when applied to the production line and handblown glass offers far more room for creativity.

These pieces are part of a commission to design a useful glass object. The steel wire frame clearly demonstrates that the glass will take the form of whatever it is restrained with. This is "a shape which grows by itself," a free-thinking experiment which produces objects of pure beauty using an organic process.

This curious, anatomical-looking object hides its true function—that of holding a lightbulb without the need for any other fixings. It explores the elasticity of glass in its heated state and the ability of the glassworker to produce forms by pushing and probing.

**Glass Object
Dimensions:
560mm x 400mm
Designer: Gijs Bakker
Client: NV Vereenigde
Glasfabrieken Leerdam**

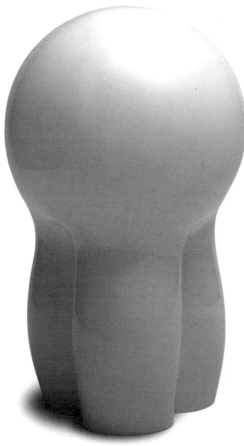

Taking shape

Key Features	Low tooling investment
	High labor costs mean expensive unit costs
	Flexible production process
	Glass can be reused and recycled
Typical Applications	All mass-produced glass drinks containers, pharmaceutical containers, and food packaging.

**Glass Lamp
Dimensions:
320mm x 170mm
Designer: Gijs Bakker
Client: NV Vereenigde
Glasfabrieken Leerdam**

Delicate threads

The true value of glass can only be fully appreciated when considering the number of forms and functions that it assumes, not just on a visual, decorative level but on microscopic and structural levels too.

Glass fiber is the collective term for glass that has been processed into thin strands. These can be divided into three product areas: glass wool or insulating glass, textile fibers, and optical fibers. Each one fulfills diverse and distinct functions within a range of industries.

Glass wool is made from soda–lime glass by the centrifugal spinning of molten glass beads into short threads and is generally used in building and loft insulation, either alone or combined with mortar or plaster. Fiberglass textiles are used in plastic reinforcement, both in injection moldings and hand lay-up work. Fiber optics are used within a range of industries to carry light. Because optical fibers can transmit light around corners, they can be applied within a diverse range of industries.

Dimensions	**Diameter can be accurately controlled to the thickness of a human hair**
Key Features	**Heat- and fire-resistant**
	Good electrical insulation
	Good strength-to-weight ratio
	Impervious to many caustics
More	**www.corning.com**
	www.schott.com
	www.cem-fil.com
	www.vetrotexeurope.com
	www.sgtf.com
Typical Applications	**Fibers can be used in glass-reinforced plastics, boat hulls, automobile bodies, and concrete glass yarn for textiles.**

076

Glass tubing is used as a starting point for many products, from domestic tableware and ornaments to ampoules and fluorescent light tubes. Using mainly lampworking, or bench- and lathe-working as two of the processes to form products, they themselves are produced by two main methods: the Danner and Vello processes.

As a semi-finished product, the glass tube is one of the main forms in which glass is bought before undergoing a secondary production process. It is available in round sections as well as an assortment of different shapes. Conturax® by Schott is a range of borosilicate inner- and outer-profiled glass tubing that can be worked into a range of products requiring a strong decorative element.

By starting with a semi-finished material the possibilities for creating small- to medium-volume production becomes an option. There are many small to large lathe-working companies that can handform the tube into products avoiding tooling costs.

Dimensions	**Tubes from 1mm–450mm in diameter**
Production	**Cast acrylic resin**
	Plastic epoxy-coated aluminum tubes
Key Features	**Good resistance to thermal shock**
	Good workability
	Resistance to corrosion
More	**www.schott.com**
	www.intracel.co.uk
	www.accu-glass.com
Typical Applications	**Fluorescent lighting, television tubes, scientific equipment, oil and vinegar bottles, thermometers, and decorative ornaments.**

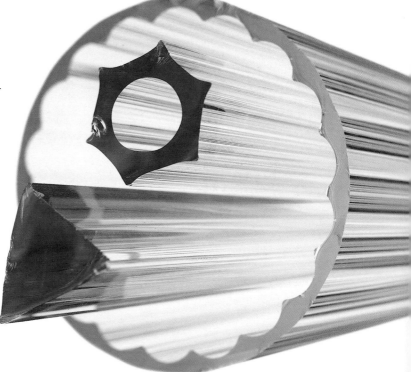

Detail of Conturax® glass tubes by Schott

Tube function

Glass balloons, fibers, strands, wool, flakes, and spheres are often combined with other materials to improve their characteristics. Glass fiber has many applications within both high- and low-tech industries: optical fibers, glass wool, and reinforcements for polymers for example.

The continuous glass fiber in Aldo Bakker's chair is common in furniture design. It is combined with a polymer resin to provide an easily workable material. This glass fiber chair was the result of an experiment using single flowing lines to define a form. The designer has used the transparent qualities of the clear resin and glass fibers to produce a piece that exploits the visual qualities of this form of glass. The chair is constructed from two molds and cut-out flat patterns of fiber built up into nine layers. Alumino-silicate glass is generally used for this type of fiber due to its chemical-resistance and high softening point. The glass fiber in this chair is a necessary structural element as well as a decorative one.

Dimensions	**810mm x 460mm**
	Average thickness: 10mm
Key Features	**Heat- and fire-resistant**
	Good electrical insulation
	Flexible when being worked; rigid when combined with resin
	Low cost tooling
	Flexible production methods
	Extremely durable
	Good strength-to-weight ratio
More	**www.fibreglass.com**
	www.jeccomposites.com
Typical Applications	**Boat hulls, automobile bodies, helmets, furniture, civil engineering, aeronautics, rail transport, architecture, and toys.**

Glass fiber chair
Designer: Aldo Bakker
Client: Self-initiated
project

Flexible glass

Pockets of air

Dimensions	Sold on three criteria: density, collapse pressure, and physical size from 15–120 microns
Key Features	Lightweight, high strength, free-flowing, and inert
	Good thermal insulation properties
More	www.3m.com
	www.pottersbeads.com
	www.fillite.com
	www.decogem.com
Typical Applications	Civil explosives, acoustic windows in submarines, silicone sealants, underbody coatings for cars, engine component covers, weight reducer and thermal barrier in paint, insulation for oil pipelines, and thermal cements.

Like glass spheres, flakes, and fibers, glass beads are used as an additive within a wide range of industries and applications, from reducing weight in aircraft paint and explosives to a thermal insulator in domestic paint. One of the early applications was in civil explosives. But it is the combination of its resistance to chemicals, its durability, and its ability to be formed into simple shapes which means it can be exploited in a whole range of applications.

As with so many materials, the production of these microspheres is one of their most interesting aspects. The raw material starts off at the top of a tower. Droplets then fall past a series of flames, being heated and expanding in the process. This free-falling results in the formation of perfectly round beads. The computer-controlled process is 100 percent efficient—every glass bubble being collected and packed at the base of the tower. Microspheres are available in a range of densities—most of which look like a fine powder when seen together.

Illustration of microscopic hollow glass beads

Unexpected

Most glass is processed into products where this hard, transparent, reflective material is at least visible, and often visually exploited in packaging, tableware, and glazing for example. However, these same properties give it a unique purpose on a microscopic scale when combined with other materials.

Glass spheres from microscopic (10 times the thinness of a human hair) to 1mm-glass balls, are used in both solid and hollow glass varieties within a range of industrial applications. These spheres range from a fine dust to granules that look like grains of salt.

Made from a number of different glass types including soda-lime and alumino-silicate, these hard, perfectly round glass beads are a natural choice for road markings as they add reflectivity, as well as being hardwearing. They improve mold shrinkage, warping, and increase viscosity within plastic-molded parts.

Dimensions	**75–850 microns**
Key Features	**Reflective**
	Good chemical-resistance
	Available in a range of sizes and shapes
	Spherical
	High thermal-resistance
	Chemically inert
	Easily processed in plastic forming machines
More	**www.pottersbeads.com**
	www.fillite.com
	www.decogem.com
Typical Applications	**Reflective road markings; fillers in plastics; as an alternative to metals for sandblasting, deburring, peening, and surface effects.**

Glass beads

Microscopic

Ultra-thin and powdery, glass flakes were originally designed to be combined with other materials to reinforce and strengthen on a structural and microscopic level.

The flat C-type borosilicate glass flakes are inert and can be very, very small. One of the main industrial applications is as a barrier coating for pipes. The flat glass flakes bond to produce a layer which, on a microscopic level, acts as an impenetrable blanket. This layering potential is also used to increase the stiffness in plastic moldings.

Because there is no set shape or direction to the flakes, they offer more support than strands of glass fibers, which tend to be long, thin, and uni-directional. However, when combined with glass fibers they can give even greater strength, toughness, and stiffness than could be obtained by using fibers or flakes alone.

Like glass spheres, glass flakes are another invisible form of glass where the structural properties fulfill a function when combined with a secondary material. However, its use on this microscopic level is not just restricted to functional applications—the company Glassflake are introducing flakes for use as a decorative surface effect.

Dimensions	**Available from Glassflake in three nominal thicknesses: 3.5–5.5microns, 1.9–2.5microns, and 1.4–1.9microns**
Key Features	**Chemically inert**
	Increases chemical-resistance
	Improves wear- and abrasion-resistance
	Reduces moisture vapor transmission
	Decorative possibilities
	Improves fire retardancy
	Improves dimensional stability
	Can lower costs of parts by reducing the amount of resin used
More	**www.glassflake.com**
Typical Applications	**As a reenforcement filler to add strength, stability, and durability; to increase fire retardancy in plastic moldings.**

Glass flakes

Super glass

Fused silica can withstand temperatures of up to 2,192°F (1,200°C) for short periods and 1,652°F (900°C) for a sustained period. This extreme ability makes it very difficult to work and very expensive. Also known as quartz glass or fused quartz, fused silica is one of the highly heat-resistant materials used in the exterior of space shuttles.

Space shuttle windows are a triple-glazed sandwich: the external and middle panes of fused silica glass have alumino-silicate internal glazing. The external fused silica layer protects the shuttle from the high temperatures generated on that all important reentry to Earth's atmosphere. The inner layer of alumino-silicate, known as the pressure pane, protects the internal cabin pressure against the vacuum of space. The fused silica middle section serves as a compromise between the pressure and heat requirements.

The 37 windows in 11 different sizes on the Orbiter shuttle are a great case study in advanced applications for special glass, a material that has been used for 7,000 years.

Key Features	Outstanding resistance to thermal shock
	Excellent resistance to high temperatures
	Good chemical resistance
	Ultra-low expansion
More	www.quartz-silica.com
	www.schott.com
Typical Applications	Space shuttle windows, furnace sight glasses, mirror blanks or astronomical telescopes, and high-energy lasers.

Space shuttle
Image courtesy of NASA

082

Self-cleaning

Dimensions	Standard sheet sizes: 6,000mm x 3,210mm
Key Features	Self-cleaning and leaves no watermarks
	Cost-effective in larger buildings
	Can be single or double glazing
	Does not weaken with age
	Can use with toughened, laminated, or bent glass
	Can only be used in exterior applications
	Neutral appearance (comparable to flat glass)
	Can be formed
More	www.activeglass.com
	www.ritec.co.uk
	ppg.com/gls_aquapel/default.htm
	www.saint-gobain-glass.com
Typical Applications	Architectural glazing, automotive, roofing, windows that cannot be opened, conservatories, and greenhouses. Suitable for most applications where UV light is present.

Self-cleaning glass
Manufacturer:
Pilkington Glass

This is the kind of material development that makes the national news when it is launched. The most appealing aspect of this self-cleaning glass is that the action of the rain falling on the glass, which you would normally curse after having just cleaned your windows, is the thing that washes the dirt away. Launched in 2001, this nonstick, Teflon version of glass has a coating that absorbs ultraviolet (UV) light to create a reaction on the surface that breaks down and loosens deposits. When it rains these deposits are simply washed away.

The coating is applied to the glass during the production of the sheets themselves, which means there is no secondary production process. Once windows have been installed, the process of self-cleaning takes several days to take effect as the coating has to absorb enough UV light to begin to work. The principal technology is several years old but it took Pilkington four years to develop it for use on large sheets of glass. These sheets can also be formed for use within the automotive industry. Its main advantages are in areas which can be difficult to access, and is most cost-effective in large buildings with reduced cleaning cycles.

Fiber optics enable light to go round corners, loop and bend, twist and wind. Among the many applications of optical fibers within modern industry, its use in communications has to be one of the most significant. The term "fiber optics" came about in 1956 and described optical glass drawn into long thin strands which could transmit electrical pulses and light.

Glass core, glass skin

In the 1960s the race was on to develop and implement the new fiber optic technology. Physicists, chemists, and engineers were all attempting to formulate and produce a type of glass with enough clarity to carry light over an initial distance of one kilometer. In 1970 Corning discovered that two types of glass were needed—a major breakthrough in the field. Fiber optics have a glass core with a silica sleeve. The purity of the core allows for light to pass unobstructed through the length of the cable. The sleeve, which has a lower refractive index, stops any light escaping.

The hair-thin glass fibers were made smaller and lighter than conventional copper and today carry staggering amounts of information—another example of glass being exploited in areas of technology that seem far removed from its more obvious qualities.

Key Features	**Flexible**
	Good light-guiding properties
	Not affected by electromagnetic interference
	Chemically inert
	Excellent size to capacity ratio for carrying information
	Generates cold light for medical applications
More	**www.corning.com**
	www.schott.com
Typical Applications	**Endoscopes and close precision work for microscopes, display areas where cold light sources are needed, traffic control lighting, and decorative domestic lighting.**

Fiber optics
Manufacturer: Corning

Another smart glass! This material changes from opaque to clear with the flick of a switch—now you see it, now you don't. It can be applied as a divider for both interior and exterior spaces, and has the potential to transform domestic and office environments. This laminated glass is made up of two layers of clear or tinted glass. An interlayer of liquid crystal film is sandwiched between them. Passing an electric current through the film excites the liquid crystals into a state where they align themselves and the glass becomes transparent. When the current is turned off the crystals relax, diffusing light in all directions and making the glass opaque again.

This kind of intelligent glazing could replace traditional windows, walls, and curtains and alter our living and working environments dramatically. Partitions made of this kind of glass allow areas to be changed from private to public and back again with the flick of a switch.

**Bombay Sapphire Fishtanks,
Heathrow Airport**

Vision control

Dimensions	Maximum sheet size: 2,800mm x 1,000mm
	Minimum sheet size: 305mm x 405mm
	Standard thicknesses: 11mm, 12mm, 14mm
	Based on Saint-Gobain's PRIVA-LITE® glass
Key Features	Instantaneous adjustable vision
	Excellent clarity in transparent state
	Low power consumption
	Can be laminated for security and soundproofing
	Can be curved
	Can be used externally
	Versatile forming process
More	www.sggprivalite.com
Typical Applications	Partitioning, doors, security, screens, transport,and museum display cases.

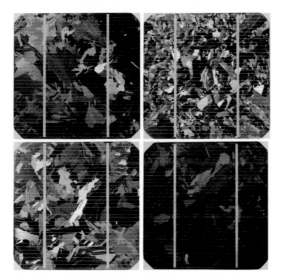

Color cells
Designer: Solar Century

Dimensions	Cells are typically 100mm–150mm²
Key Features	**Large range of decorative possibilities**
	Suitable for structural applications
	Fully compliant with fire safety standards
	Can incorporate a wide range of glass
More	**www.solarcentury.com**
Typical Applications	**Building facades, canopies, shading systems, atriums, louvers, and roof tiles.**

In a single day the sun can generate enough electricity to power the world for several years. The use of solar panels is already widespread as a replacement for constantly diminishing fossil fuels. There are many companies specializing in solar panels, but what makes these products so special is the decorative as well as functional potential they offer.

Solar Century specializes in photovoltaic technology for applications in domestic and industrial markets. Their products not only offer incredible potential for buildings to harness a renewable energy source, but also boast a range of decorative effects. The laminated panels of opaque and semi-transparent finishes can incorporate many colors from metallic silver, bronze, and gold to basic red, green, and magenta.

The flakes are formed from crystals grown using a polycrystalline method. The color comes from varying the thickness of the anti-reflective coating. Blue, for example, has the thickest anti-reflective coating, which in turn is the most efficient. Silver has the thinnest coating and is the least efficient. These panels can also be used in roofing where the cells act as a shade to reduce solar heat gain.

Astro Power AP-120 modules in the solar wall of the Big Brother House, London
Designer: Solar Century

Light and electricity

086

Dimensions	420mm x 420mm
Key Features	**Cost-effective**
	Holds panels together when broken
	Fire-resistant properties
More	**www.glaverbel.com**
	www.saint-gobain-glass.com
	Jhan Stanley, London, UK;
	Tel: +44 (0)207 377 5501
Typical Applications	**Doors, windows, overhead glazing, furniture, partitions, and fire-resistant panels.**

With its distinctive mesh and rough, textured surface one cannot escape the suggestions of industry that wire-reinforced glass provokes. However, this sandwich of rolled glass (or cast glass) and embedded wire occupies a unique position within glazing. Its traditional use is in applications where strength and security are of major importance. Its ability to remain in one piece when smashed has a particular use in roofing where objects falling on to the glass do not result in a shower of glass underneath. With the use of rolled glass and its lack of true clarity, this product offers a cost-effective alternative to laminates.

Forming the wired glass sandwich involves a continuous ribbon of molten glass, half the thickness of the final sheet, being squeezed through rollers over which the layer of wire is applied. A second layer of glass is then added to form the sandwich, which is compressed before being annealed. Wired glass is available in a range of patterns and differently sized mesh.

Taking materials out of their traditional context into different settings is a common theme. Jhan Stanley takes her inspiration from everyday found and discarded objects. She uses paper plates, plastic cups, and cutlery for inspiration, and through changing the material finds new contexts for these products.

Security blanket

Georgian Wire Square
Designer: Jhan Stanley
Client: Self-initiated project

The origin of the glass-backed mirror lies in the canals of sixteenth-century Venice where flat glass was backed with mercury and tin. To make a mirror, a sheet of glass is coated with a stannous chloride solution to prepare it for silvering. The reflective surface is made up of a blend of silver nitrate, ammonia, caustic soda, and distilled water which forms a coating of just 0.01mm. Once dry a protective layer can be applied to protect the mirror surface.

Rebecca Newnham's appreciation of mirrors is built on their ability to not only reflect an image, but also to play with light by reflecting it on to interior and exterior surfaces and interacting with the environment. She designs to commission for interiors and exteriors.

Dimensions	**1,000mm diameter**
More	**www.rebeccanewnham.co.uk**
	www.saint-gobain-glass.com
Typical Applications	**Decorative and functional domestic mirrors, mirrors in telescopes, camera lenses, and sunglasses.**

More than reflection

Zen 1 Mirror
Designer: Rebecca Newnham

Silvery effects on a flat sheet, with a deceptive depth of color and texture—these are the light-changing qualities that give Dichrolam'™ its special-effect personality. When John Blazy was working with dichroic glass he found that it had certain physical limitations. His desire for a new material made this designer turn chemist to produce Dichrolam™. This unique material is made up of hundreds of layers of polymer sheets sandwiched between two layers of glass. This stack of layers takes incoming white light and separates the colors by reflecting back certain color wavelengths so that a series of 3D textured patterns can be seen. Dichrolam™ has been used in light panels, which change color as you walk past, as well as conference tables for MTV.

Dimensions	2,370mm lengths in 950mm and 1,175mm widths
	Thickness from 5mm–25mm
Key Features	Can be fabricated like any laminated glass sheet
	Interior and exterior use
	A fraction of the cost of dichroic glass
	Distinctive 3D pattern
More	www.johnblazydesigns.com
	www.vitglass.com
Typical Applications	Flooring, partition walls, furniture, lighting, wall tiles, architectural glass panels, table and bar tops, diffractors for light fixtures, and shower doors.

3D image, 2D surface

Black Sea Dichrolam™ sample

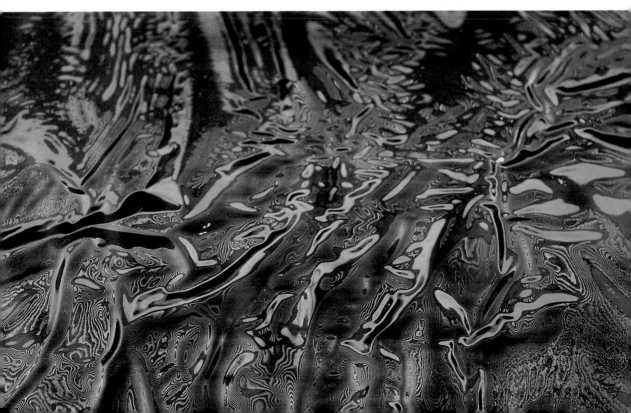

Dimensions	AF45, D263 T flat panel display glass in standard sheet sizes of 440mm x 360mm
	Alternative sizes can be produced to order
	AF45 0.045mm–1.1mm; D263 0.03mm–1.1mm
Key Features	Extremely thin
	Flexible
	Superior flatness
	Chemically-resistant
	Good surface for coatings
	Good thermal-resistance
More	www.schott.com
	www.schottglass.co.uk
Typical Applications	Can be used in flat TV screens, cellphones, pagers, PDAs, watches, opto-electronic components, glass wafers for temperature sensors, PALC displays, and electronic toys.

World's thinnest glass

Extremes are always interesting. Schott is just one of the companies that produce flat panel display glass, and appear to hold the record for the thinnest glass in the world, which measures in at just 0.03mm. This paper-thin glass is so thin that it bends like a plastic film.

Pushing technology in one area has had the knock-on effect of related industries having to push their own boundaries of development. Super-thin flat panel display glass is one example. The increasing miniaturization of handheld electronic products requires ultra-thin borosilicate glass for greater optical clarity and scratch resistance over polymer alternatives. Schott produce three main types of display glass which are differentiated by their alkaline content and thermal expansion rates.

One of the surprising features of this type of glass is its flexibility which allows it to be formed into curved screens. It is widely used in touch-screen displays.

**Sample of flat panel
display glass from Schott**

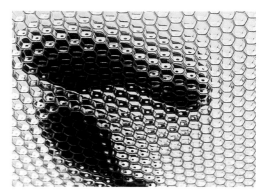

Glass and aluminum
panel sample
Manufacturer: Cellbond
Architectural

Kaleidoscopic

As far as panel products go this kaleidoscopic material has to be one of the most visually interesting. Float glass, aluminum, and resin combine to create the hollow honeycomb cells, giving a greater strength-to-weight ratio than standard glass-only sheet materials.

These honeycomb cells also create a fly's-eye view by distorting the light and deforming the world into a series of tiny apertures, giving it a unique aesthetic potential. A range of colors and surface finishes can be specified to enhance this effect or used for more practical applications such as nonslip flooring.

Cellbond Architectural produce composite panels using rigid honeycomb cell structures bonded between a range of materials. These panels exploit the hardness, transparency, and scratch-resistance of glass within interior and architectural applications to produce a totally unique visual experience. It is the seeing but not recognizing that suggests potential for situations where light but also privacy is needed.

Dimensions	Any size to order up to 3,000mm x 1,500mm
	Thickness: 25mm–50mm
Key Features	Strong, lightweight, and rigid
	Range of sizes and thickness
	Available in any color
	Matte or gloss finish
	Highly unique decorative quality
	Available in a range of surfaces
More	www.cellbond.net
Typical Applications	Suitable for flooring, banisters, doors, screening, partitioning, light diffusion, exhibition stands, and suspended ceilings.

Dimensions	From 210mm x 297mm up to any size; up to 100mm deep
More	Ruth Spaak, Glass for Interiors, Stratford-upon-Avon, UK Tel: +44 (0)1789 415244
Typical Applications	Window features, blinds, screens, room dividers (best seen against a window), and interior screening.

Materials medley

Ruth Spaak was originally a constructed textile designer, but after retraining in glass she discovered a particular working method which is a unique marriage of the two. She produces a range of pieces, which are literally a fusion of glass with other materials.

She begins by hand, cutting tiny pieces of glass into squares, circles, and rectangles using a basic glasscutter. This is the most time-consuming part of the process but offers the most rewards. "The making is like playing, the making up is pure pleasure—that's the best bit," says Spaak. The hundreds of tiny pieces are laid on a special paper that stops the glass from sticking to the kiln when heated.

Heating and fusing gives each piece a smooth, fire-polished edge. The fused pieces can then be stitched, knotted, and tied together using a range of found objects, from cables to latex rubber. The clear glass is the most important element in each piece, and, when combined with the color and texture of other materials, gives glittery, harsh, and transparent visual effects.

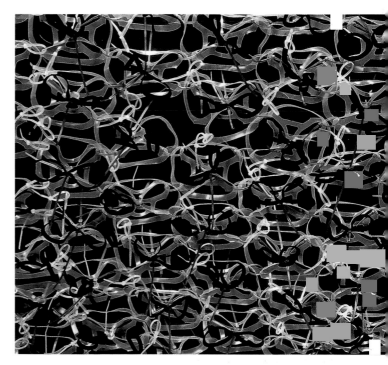

Lace Construction
Designer: Ruth Spaak

Dimensions	Total thickness: 38.7mm; average area: 18,500mm
	Panels vary: 800mm x 1,500mm and 2,200mm x 3,300mm
Key Features	Excellent thermal and sound insulation
	Cavities can incorporate secondary materials
	Can incorporate decorative elements
	Available double or triple glazed
	Can be made from clear, body-tinted, annealed, toughened, or laminated glass
More	www.daylight.uk.com
	www.okalux.de
	www.fosterandpartners.com
Typical Applications	Sloping and vertical structures; bolted, suspended assemblies.

Glass ceiling

There are three main types of double glazing: mass-produced, low specification windows for domestic and office buildings; architectural glass with special coatings; and highly specialized applications such as curved glass, or panels with functioning cavities. The glass used in the Great Court of the British Museum fits into the second area. The predominant feature is the glass roof. The minute you walk into this luxurious space you can't help but marvel at the delicate, organic steel lattice grid of the roof structure.

The use of glass in this structure is important due to the processing, logistics, and creativity of the project, rather than the type of glass that was specified. Each of the 3,312 differently sized, CNC-cut, Okatherm units has three coatings. The main function of all these coatings is to reduce the solar energy and amount of direct sun penetrating the building, while still letting daylight in— they prevent over 75 percent of the sun's heat from ever entering the court.

**The British Museum's
Great Court
Designer: Norman
Foster and Partners
Client: British Museum**

Animated

Visual Impact Technology produces a range of laminated glass with a truly animated visual effect—an optical techno light show.

This is made possible by a patented interlayer system sandwiched between two pieces of clear, tinted, annealed, float, or tempered glass. One of the major advantages this type of holographic glass has over other holographic decorative panels is its transparency. What you see is a totally clear sheet, with a range of decorative holographic patterns in the surface. Although logos and other specific designs can be made to order, there is a good range of standard patterns to choose from.

This marriage of light and technology allows for unique ornamentation on glass panels which can be treated in the same way as standard laminated glass products. As with all holographic images it is difficult to appreciate the qualities of the glass without seeing it first hand as the effect changes according to the angle it is viewed from and the direction of reflected light—a real attention-grabber.

Dimensions	**Maximum size: 1,000mm x 3,000mm**
	Up to 25.4mm thick
Key Features	**High decorative potential**
	Bespoke designs can be produced
	Internal and external applications
	Can incorporate other functional interlayers
	Can be treated in the same way as normal laminated glass
More	**www.vitglass.com**
Typical Applications	**Suitable for use in room dividers, walls, furniture, shower screens, ceiling tiles, conference tables, wash basin inlays, hand rails, insulated units, signages, and escalator partitions.**

**Holographic glass
Manufacturer: Vitglass**

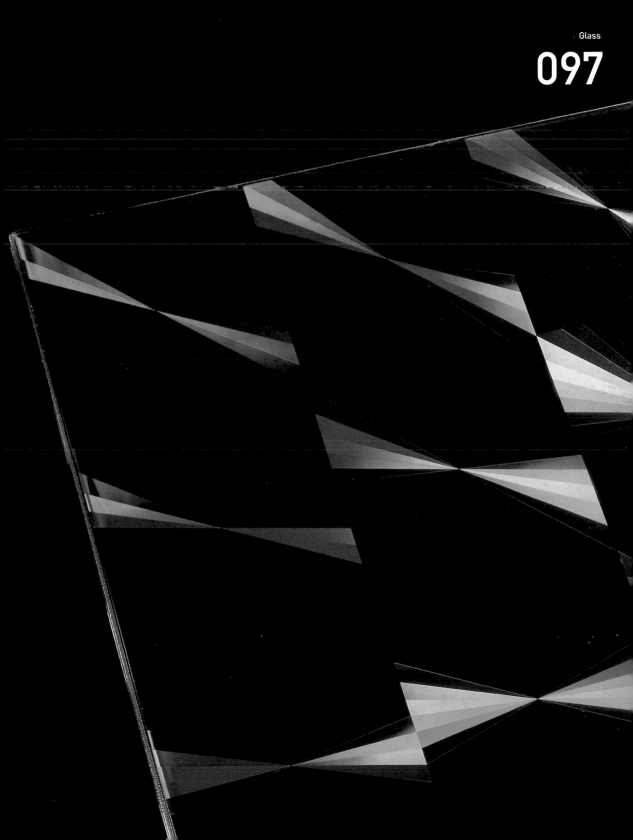

Tiny squares of glass positioned closely together is one of the oldest techniques used for decorating on a large scale. The challenge now is to produce fresh, interesting designs in a different way within new contexts.

Making mosaics is one of the most accessible methods of producing a glass object. There is no heat involved, no expensive molds or tooling, and no machines for grinding or polishing. The skill is in the ability to visualize and interpret a surface and pattern made up of hundreds of small pieces of glass. It is also a method of using glass where there is no limit to the scale. There are two methods of producing mosaic designs: the indirect and the direct method.

Making and installing a mosaic piece—the indirect method:

• First design the motif defining the colors and key areas.
• Collect the colored glass.
• Draw your design on to a large sheet of brown paper. Stick the glass on to the paper using glue.
• Cut the paper into manageable sections which can be taken on-site.
• Press the glass directly into an adhesive on the surface you want to mosaic.
• When dry, soak the paper and remove.

The direct method speaks for itself as the pattern is laid directly on to the surface on-site by a skilled craftsman.

**Mosaic samples
Designers: Mosaik,
Pierre Mesguish**

Unlimited scale

Key Features	**Durable**
	Highly decorative
Typical Applications	**Common uses include flooring, walls, decorative panels, shower-screens, decoration in nightclubs and bathrooms, kitchen splashbacks, floors, swimming pools, ornamental pools, company logos, and table tops.**

New materials, new fastening techniques, new applications! The All Glass Bridge captures the imagination by using a new material according to an ancient principle. There are many designs where glass is an integral part of the structure—but the All Glass Bridge is unique, and, as the name proclaims, uses no other material.

The idea for a 100 percent glass structure originated at the Thomas Heatherwick Studio in 1996. The concept rests on using 4,000 pieces of 8mm water-jet, clear, toughened glass. Strength is achieved by bonding the edges of the pieces together using a specially developed UV adhesive—one that does not deteriorate with prolonged exposure to direct sunlight.

The basic arch shape provides a nonslip surface but no grip. The solution was to place each piece of glass at a slightly different height to the next, leaving each corner exposed. From the handrail to the fixings, this is a structure that exploits the physical qualities of glass and the supreme strength of UV-bonding.

Dimensions	24,000mm x 6,000mm
Key Features	**Exceptional strength**
	Invisible joints
More	**www.thomasheatherwick.com**
Typical Applications	**Furniture, drinks bottles, glazing, and interior shop fittings.**

Super-strong bonding

All Glass Bridge
Designers: Thomas
Heatherwick Studio, Anthony
Hunt Associates, and Lighting
Design Partnership
Client: Self-initiated project

Michael Anastassiades' mirrored products are curious and captivating. Inspired by vacuum flasks, he has taken the familiar and established process of mirroring and applied it to a range of domestic products. The objects are made from handmade blown glass and lathe-worked borosilicate tubing.

For the shot glasses, glass is blown into one mold to make the outside shape; it is then taken to another mold, which creates the internal form. Once the glass has been cut, leaving an open end, a silver nitrate solution is poured into the cavity. A few minutes later, the silver is deposited on to the glass and the solution can be poured away. Once the silver coating is dry it will corrode if left exposed to the air. To prevent this, a mirrored disc is glued on the underside to create an airtight seal.

Traditional mirroring production involves the application of a number of coatings to stop the silver corroding. A series of experiments led to varnish being used to protect the surface of the mirrored vases and lampshades.

Dimensions	**250mm x 85mm; 370mm x 100mm; 500mm x 100mm**
Production	**Silvered on to blown and lathe-worked glassware**
Key Features	**Good insulation properties**
	Decorative finish
	Low to medium tooling
More	**www.michaelanastassiades.com**
Typical Applications	**Scientific instruments, vacuum flasks, mirrors, and jewelry.**

**Mirror Vases
Designer: Michael
Anastassiades
Client: Babylon**

Reflections

The use of glass beads is a common way of getting road markings to reflect light. The difference with this product is that the markings continue to glow once the car has passed. Traditional road reflectors only work when the powerful beam of a car headlamp is shining directly on to them.

Glass beads are hardwearing, cost-effective, and reflective, and benefit pedestrians, animals, and cyclists as well as cars. This technology has been around for some time but the major obstacle to wider use has been the cost of the phosphorescent powder and mixing it with paint. Product 2000 have overcome this by coating the beads. There is no need for baking as the powder is held on to the beads when they are sprinkled and pushed on to the soft surface of the thermoplastic paint—trapping the powder between the sphere and the paint. Ironically, the glass beads are generally made from shattered car windscreens.

Glow in the dark

Key Features	Benefits pedestrians, animals, and drivers
	Hardwearing
	Cost-effective compared with traditional road reflectors
	No power is needed to generate light
	Safe, nontoxic coating
More	www.pottersbeads.com
	Product 2000; Tel: +44 (0)1425 652226
Typical Applications	Garages, warehouses, fire escapes, edges of platforms on railway stations, airports, and aircraft interiors.

Phosphorescent-coated road markings

Dimensions	**170mm x 300mm x 6mm thickness**
Key Features	**Varying degrees of translucency**
	Emits a greenish-yellow light lasting approximately one hour
	Good weathering-resistance
	Creates a 2D pattern during the day and a 3D effect in darkness
More	**www.gruppe-re.de**
	www.rctritec.com
Typical Applications	**Interiors, swimming pools, architectural glazing, facades, windows, and doors.**

Onda glass tiles
Designers: Nicole Huttner
and Silke Warchold
Client: Experimental

Gruppe RE are two designers interested in finding new applications for existing materials and technology. Inspired by the phosphorescent ink found in plastic security and safety applications, they have produced a unique design for glass tiles, which takes this ink coating into new territories.

The tiles offer an alternative to the more common ceramic variety by allowing a greater depth of color possibilities. The screen-printing process they use involves three glass enamels: a first layer of illuminating ink, a second layer of red, and a third layer of turquoise. The three colored enamels are screen-printed on to clear glass tiles and burnt on to the surface at 1,202–1,328°F (650–720°C) for two to four minutes, to create a surface with a lasting resilience. Clear Optiwhite glass had to be used for the tiles as the green tint common in most glazing applications acts as a UV-barrier, preventing absorption of UV light.

This multilayering creates depth so that in daylight the translucent ink allows the red and turquoise to come through, and in the dark only the phosphorescent element can be seen.

Luminous

Dimensions	905mm x 625mm x 600mm
Production	**Cast acrylic resin**
	Plastic epoxy-coated aluminum tubes
Key Features	**Removable and easy to install**
	Cost-effective and low maintenance
	Decorative and functional applications
More	**www.madico.com**
Typical Applications	**Shop windows, office partitioning, furniture, and doors.**

Window dressing

Curtains and blinds seem old-fashioned compared with the range of thin plastic films now available that can transform windows and archictectural glass. From plain acid-etched textures, colored films, and mirrored effects to films that will appear clear from one angle and opaque from another, glass is going glam. These surfaces can be applied just as easily as they can be replaced.

One of the key advantages of these films is in their ability to dress or undress a window or partition according to changing functions. Because they can be applied directly on-site, films can be removed and replaced at any time. They also allow for complete creative freedom for designing and cutting out specific shapes. But these films are not restricted to decorative applications either—some films can control solar heat gain in buildings and enhance shatter-resistance.

Opalux® privacy screening film with decorative cut-out

105 Metal

Flow

Manhole covers easily blend into the
background of our everyday environments,
rarely noticed or given a second thought by
most of us. One of the key features of cast
iron and the reason for its prolific use for so
many years is its exceptional fluidity, and its
ability to take on complex, intricate shapes.
Cast iron is the generic name for a group
of materials made from carbon, silicon,
and iron. A high carbon content ensures
good flow characteristics during casting,
and is present in two forms, graphite and
iron carbide.

The presence of graphite in cast iron gives
manhole covers their excellent wear-
resistance. Rust is generally superficial and
is constantly polished off by wear. However,
to deter rust, the castings are covered with
a bitumen coating which fuses with the
porous iron. This traditional process of
producing sand-cast materials is being used
by many contemporary designers in more
and more exciting new applications.

Dimensions	**810mm diameter x 100mm deep**
Key Features	**Excellent fluidity**
	Cost-effective
	Good wear-resistance
	Low solidification shrinkage
	Brittle
	Good compression strength
	Good machinability
More	**www.karimrashid.com**
Typical Applications	**Cast iron has been used for hundreds of years in buildings, bridges, engineering components, furniture, and kitchenware.**

**Millennium manhole
cover for New York City
Designer: Karim Rashid
Client: Con Edison**

Cylinda line hot water jug
(right), and Cylinda line
teapot (below)
Designer: Arne Jacobson
Manufacturer: Stelton

New domestic landscape

The evolution of tableware provides us with a useful history of our materials and production methods, with metal taking center stage. Metal objects fall into two broad categories: firstly, we have basic, simple tools, created for necessity of function; secondly, we have the more ostentatious, ornamental, silver, and gold artifacts. The development of mass-production techniques and the industrial revolution provided an opportunity for the basic and the ostentatious to coincide, and new materials gave designers the chance to revolutionize our domestic landscape.

There are four major types of stainless steel: austenitic, ferritic, ferritic–austenitic (duplex), and martensitic. The stainless steel used in domestic applications is generally austenitic. Stelton, founded in 1960, are well known for their iconic, brushed stainless steel designs. Virtually all the products from this manufacturer boast a functional aesthetic; the clean, cylindrical, functional forms are as much to do with choice of material as the design. The combination of quality stainless steel and high production values raises these Stelton products to luxury status.

Dimensions	**Teapot 130mm high; hot water jug 125mm high**
Key Features	**Hygienic**
	Noncorrosive
	Capable of an outstanding surface finish
	Excellent toughness
	Can be formed using a variety of processes
	Difficult to coldwork
More	**www.stelton.com**
Typical Applications	**Austenitic stainless steel is used in housewares, industrial piping, and architecture. Martensitic stainless steel is used to make knives and turbine blades. Ferritic stainless steel is corrosion-resistant and is used for internal components in washing machines and boilers. Duplex stainless steel is highly corrosion-resistant and is used in aggressive environments.**

Ring My Bell schoolbells
Designer: Olof Kolte
Design
Client: Skultuna
Messingsbruk

Musical metals

Brass is an alloy of copper (approximately 65 percent) and zinc (no more than 40 percent). The mechanical properties and characteristics of brass vary dramatically depending on the alloy and working method. There are around 70 different brass alloys, most of which can be grouped into major families. The most common are straight brasses, which have a zinc content of between five and 40 percent. Some of the brasses in this group include jewelry bronze, red brass, yellow brass, and gilding metal. Other main brass groups include leaded brass, casting brasses, and tin brasses. Some brasses are known as bronzes. Bronze is a copper alloy that has a main alloying element other than the usual zinc or nickel.

These schoolbells by Swedish manufacturer Skultana Messingsbruk exploit the long musical tradition of brass. They have nearly 400 years of experience in forming handcrafted brass objects and a product range that reflects this history as well as contemporary, functional design.

Dimensions	**160mm height; 460g weight**
Key Features	**Versatility in production**
	Recyclable
	Good machinability
	Good corrosion-resistance
	Good hotworking properties
	Good combination of strength and ductility
More	**www.brass.org**
	www.skultuna.com
Typical Applications	**A variety of brass alloys are used in a large number of applications including electric plugs; lightbulb fittings; precision medical instruments; cable glands; bearings; gearwheels; household and plumbing fittings; and aircraft, train, and car components.**

Dimensions	Seat 580mm wide; 2,440mm wide overall
Key Features	Low unit cost
	Allows for production of thin walls
	High rate of production
	High tooling costs
	High tolerance
More	www.omkdesign.co.uk
Typical Applications	Camera bodies and housings for electronic and engine components.

This simple seating design is based on three main elements: the seat, the support brackets, and a supporting triangular beam. The striking simplicity of this system is a great example of the possibilities of cast aluminum, which exploits the design of a single structural element, which can then be reproduced in multiples. Rodney Kinsman says the design was inspired by an aircraft wing with a stressed skin structure.

The basic chair design can remain as just that, or it can act as a skeleton onto which other materials can be added. The surface

Component furniture

Trax seating system
Designer: Rodney Kinsman
Manufacturer: OMK Design

can be easily washed down and has a maximum resistance to wear and tear. The simplicity of this set of components also allows for economical assembly.

Die-casting, sand-casting, and investment casting are all common methods used to produce metal components. Die-casting produces identical complex shapes and uses low temperature metals like aluminum, zinc, and magnesium. Molten metal is forced under high pressure into a water-cooled metal die. When the component is solid, the pressure is released and the component ejected.

Profile designs

Extrusion is another common process applied to a range of metallic and nonmetallic materials. The key aspect of this manufacturing process is that it allows you to produce a long strip of a profile, which can then be sliced into the desired lengths. Aluminum is a popular material for extrusions, as it has a low melting point. This is an essential characteristic of all extrusion materials, which include copper, stainless steels, medium and low carbon steels, and magnesium.

Extrusion is often combined with other methods, for example, extrusion blow molding for plastics, or impact extrusion for metals. For standard metal extrusion however, there are two main forms: direct extrusion, where the metal is forced through a stationary die, allowing for longer lengths to be produced; and indirect extrusion, where the die compresses the metal producing less friction but shorter lengths.

Dimensions	**2,250mm wide overall**
Key Features	**Allows for production of long, continuous lengths of the same shape**
	Allows for both solid and hollow shapes
	Low cost
	Can be applied to a range of materials
More	**www.hydro.com**
	www.omkdesign.co.uk
	www.aec.org
Typical Applications	**The process is universal and can be applied to most areas of design and engineering, including tubing, sheet materials, structures and body frames for motor vehicles, furniture, and components for consumer electronics.**

Saville Bench
Designer: Rodney Kinsman
Manufacturer: OMK Design

Evolution

Nambe products are made from a combination of state-of-the-art technology and basic sand-casting methods. These salt and pepper pots are made from an aerospace-mixed aluminum alloy first produced in 1949. There is no silver, so it never tarnishes, and no lead, so it never cracks and is food safe. It stays polished with little upkeep and is 100 percent recyclable, as all metals separate at different temperatures.

"Each piece of Nambe is handled by 16 different people to produce the high-quality finished product. In 1994, the company introduced new technology in an attempt to reduce their costs and reach a greater market. But because Nambe was renowned for its handcrafted range, production methods had to combine the old and the new technologies. In the US, Nambe has revolutionized the tabletop industry and is now a market leader selling to Bloomingdales, Macy's, museum shops, and the finest tabletop retailers," says designer Karim Rashid.

Dimensions	**127.5mm high**
Key Features	**High strength-to-weight ratio**
	Easily forms alloys
	Excellent corrosion-resistance
	Excellent heat and electricity conductor
	Ductile
	Recyclable
More	**www.karimrashid.com**
	www.nambe.com
Typical Applications	**Aluminum alloy casting has applications in a huge range of products, from industrial components to tableware and giftware.**

Kissing salt and pepper pots
Designer: Karim Rashid
Client: Nambe

Flexible production

The starting point for this project was the idea of producing an inexpensive gift for lovers. The Adam & Eve keyrings, which slot together, are packaged in a glass chemistry bottle. The packaging is not only an intrinsic part of the narrative—i.e. the chemistry of lovers—but it can also be recycled. The design is based on male and female lavatory symbols with two "carefully-placed" slots which allow the keyrings to come together at any time. Adam & Steve and Anna & Eve keyrings are also available.

"The keyrings are made by laser-cutting— a process that needs a relatively small amount of initial tooling investment and offers a flexible production process. You can use laser-cutting to make 10 or a million pieces. It's a good method of cutting out complex or intricate shapes. Originally, I wanted to use stainless steel but it proved to be cheaper to use plain steel and electroplate it with nickel. Nickel has a good resistance to tarnishing and corrosion maintaining that bright shiny surface which actually can also be applied to plastics," says designer Ben Panayi.

Dimensions	46mm x 32mm
Key Features	**Flexible production**
	No post-production finishing
	Intricate shapes can be cut
	Suitable for a range of materials
More	**b.panayi@blueyonder.co.uk**
Typical Applications	**Intricate and fine patterns can be laser-cut into many flat materials. It is impossible to limit the use of laser-cutting to a specific group of products. It is used to cut a diverse range of materials—from plastic and ceramics to wood and glass—within many different engineering and domestic applications.**

Adam & Eve Keyrings
Designer: Ben Panayi
Manufacturer: Purves & Purves

Material culture is littered with examples of materials that break with convention. That is to say, they are bent, formed, twisted, and heated into forms that contradict the preconceived nature of their physical qualities. They offer unexpected shapes that you might normally expect of another material. These pieces by designer Stephen Newby boast that surprising quality—the result of inflating a metal.

These soft pillow shapes are in stark contrast to the tough quality of the steel they are made from. The process, which has a patent pending, involves inflating the stainless steel without molds. Each inflated piece responds in a different way, resulting in a unique design. The company produces a range of architectural and interior products where the material takes on a new language—not hard and rigid as you might expect, but much softer and more flexible, like a normal pillow.

Inflatable steel

Dimensions	**180mm² x 50mm deep**
Key Features	**Unique processing method for metals**
	Can be applied to a range of sizes (limited by sheet size only)
	One-off or batch-production
	Limitless shaping possibilities
More	**www.fullblownmetals.com**
Typical Applications	**Architectural, interiors, domestic accessories, furniture, and tableware.**

**Plug container in
polished stainless steel
Designer: Stephen Newby**

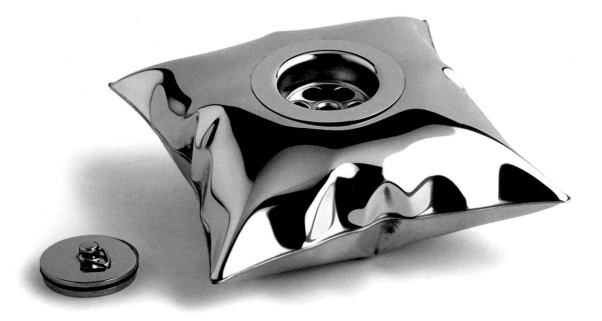

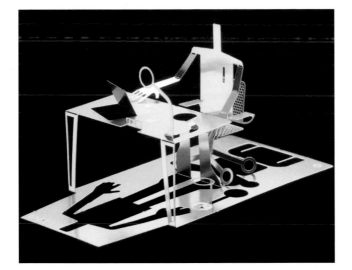

Cutting and folding a flat sheet of material to form a product is a traditional design method. This process has the potential to create paper-thin, delicate, and intricate, yet rigid patterns on the surface of the material.

Sam Buxton has created an alternative business card: "I originally used acid-etched, stainless steel cards for my business. I was interested in the idea of each card being something to keep on your desk. I also liked the idea of making miniature scenes from a flat sheet. A manufacturer saw the cards and asked me to make a series that could be mass-produced. Stainless steel was the best material to use because it was rigid, held its shape, and, when combined with the technology, was a perfect way of realizing this piece of theater."

Buxton draws the image on a CAD program, then sends it in digital format to the manufacturer. They then make a photographic screen, which is used to print an acid-resistant ink onto both sides of the steel because the acid will eat away at the metal from either side, reducing the time it needs to stay in the acid bath. It also means that patterns can be formed without cutting the steel all the way through. Acid-etching provides a much more cost-effective way of cutting intricate patterns in metals than processes like laser-cutting.

Chemical milling

Dimensions	**80mm² x 80mm thickness unfolded; 0.15mm stainless steel**
Key Features	**High tolerance**
	Thinnest bar is 0.2mm
	Thinnest line is 0.04mm
	Any flat shape can be used
	One-offs or mass-production
	Low-cost tooling
	Suitable for photographic images
	Considerably cheaper than laser-cutting
More	**www.mikroworld.com**
	www.npw.co.uk
Typical Applications	**Screens for printing solder tracks onto PC boards within the electronics industry, industrial components, and flexible trigger devices for missiles (the fine trigger changes according to air pressure the closer it gets to its target).**

Mikro Man House
Designer: Sam Buxton
Distributor: Worldwide

Rigid origami

Twist it, paint it, wrap it, stick it, and it will always hold its shape. Photographers and film studio technicians use this incredible material for reducing unwanted spill from light. By folding and creasing this sheet material around lighting, they have more control over its effect. It also has the advantage of not burning under the intense heat of studio lights.

A sheet of BLACKWRAP feels like a cross between a thick aluminum kitchen foil and paper. It is more rigid than foil and has a matte finish due to the black paint. It is an excellent material for simple forming with a unique tactile experience.

Dimensions	600mm x 7,500mm; 300mm x 15,000mm
Key Features	Heat-resistant
	Very pliable
	Keeps its shape
	Blocks light
More	www.lemarkgroup.co.uk
	www.gamonline.com
	www.allfoils.com
Typical Applications	BLACKWRAP is good for masking light leaks in technical lighting applications such as film and photography studios. It is also used to black-out windows and conceal cabling.

Sample of **BLACKWRAP**
Distributed in the US by
Gam Products Inc.

Skin

Need to replace one of your grandmother's silver plates, or perhaps produce your own intricately-patterned design in silver? Consider electroforming, a process that goes one step further than electroplating. Instead of producing a layer of only a few microns thick, electroforming builds up a skin of metal of even thickness which is then thick enough to be lifted off the mold.

The process electro-deposits metal onto molds or mandrels. When a sufficient build-up of metal is achieved, the component is separated from the mold. These molds can be made from any nonconductive material, which can be coated with conductive coating prior to plating. The cost of electroforming is based on the amount of metal used—i.e. the surface area of the mold and the thickness of the deposited metal.

With most other methods of manufacture, the material to be used is transformed from one state to another, but with electroforming a replica is created by the slow build-up of a skin over the mold. Intricate, flat, and 3D patterns can easily be reproduced without expensive tooling. It is also unique in that it creates a uniform layer around the mold, unlike pressing, which stretches the material and creates an uneven thickness.

Brass trumpet bell
Produced by: BJS Electroforming

Dimensions	350mm long
Key Features	Excellent definition in detailing
	Produces uniform thickness
	Low tooling costs
	Easy to replicate existing products
	High tolerance
More	www.bjsco.com
Typical Applications	Electroforming is an economical way of reproducing designs that are intricately patterned without a large investment in tooling. Many highly decorated Victorian silver tableware pieces were produced using this technique. Today, it is used for technical laboratory apparatus, musical instruments, and highly detailed silverware.

Dimensions	Approximately 30mm long when unformed
Key Features	Shape-altering
	Available in a range of forms, shapes, and products
	Corrosion-resistant
	Bio-compatible
More	www.memory-metalle.de
	www.memry.com
	www.fraunhofer.de
	www.nidi.org
Typical Applications	Thermal memory effects are used in areas where movement needs to take place in a restricted space. Most applications are in engineering where it is used for tube-coupling in spacecrafts, actuators in a range of industrial applications, on/off switches, and thermostats.

Nitinol thermal shape
memory alloy paperclip
Manufacturer: Memory-
Metalle GmbH

Welcome to the world of shape memory alloys. With these materials, you enter the arena of smart materials: those which respond to an external stimulus or, in less formal terms, that are worthy of their own magic show.

Imagine a straight strip of metal that, when heated, or has an electrical current passed through it, will transform itself into a paper clip, or a superelastic metal that can be twisted and bent and then relax and return to its original form. Collectively, these materials are known as shape memory alloys: materials that have been given a memory.

There are several varieties of shape memory alloys. Memory-Metalle is a leading producer of these nickel-titanium metals. Thermal shape memory alloys respond to heat, transforming them from one shape to another, which the metal is programmed to remember. This transformation is fully reversible, allowing the alloy to return to its original shape if distorted. This means that you can bend and twist the metal, heat it, and watch it return to its original shape.

Memory

Dimensions	203mm length; 25mm thickness
Key Features	Good insulation
	High strength-to-weight ratio
	100 percent recyclable
	Highly distinctive, decorative surface
	Can be post-formed using heat
More	www.alusion.com
	www.cymat.com
Typical Applications	Alusion is used in a variety of interior applications including flooring, interior accessories, signage, countertops, and lighting.

Imagine a porous and lightweight natural sponge, but instead of being soft and squashy as you would expect, it is rigid and hard, like an eroded, rough-textured piece of metallic rock, or even a metallic wasps' nest.

Alusion's stabilized aluminum foam is different from other metallic foams: it is more rugged and does not have the regularity of sponge-like pores. The company uses a patented process to produce a range of sheet products that exploit the lightweight properties of open cells. Ceramic particles are added to an aluminum alloy to form the basic material. The foam is created when gas bubbles enter the molten material. The foam then collects on the surface, where it is continuously drawn off to form a sheet.

The sheets are available in two densities with different cell sizes and a range of finishes, including glass and resin. With a texture as rough as brick, and a surface that allows pockets of light to filter through, this is a unique material to add to the designer's palette of semi-formed sheet materials.

Designer holes

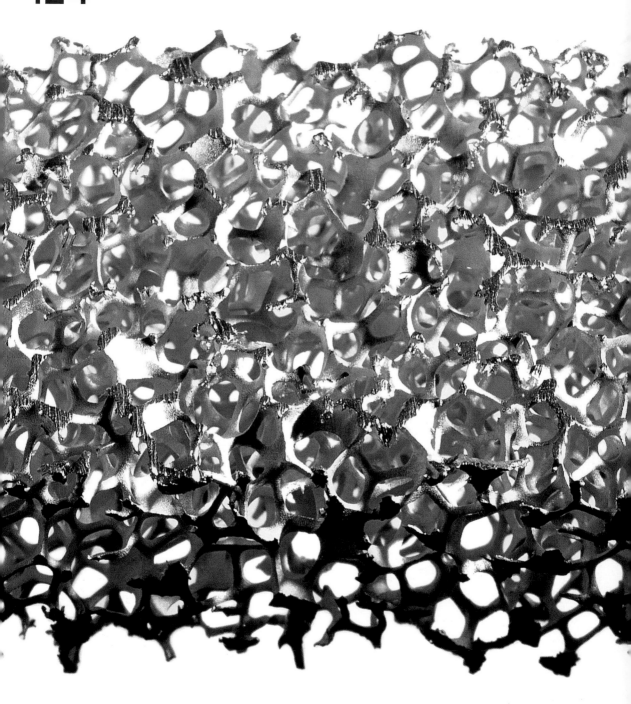

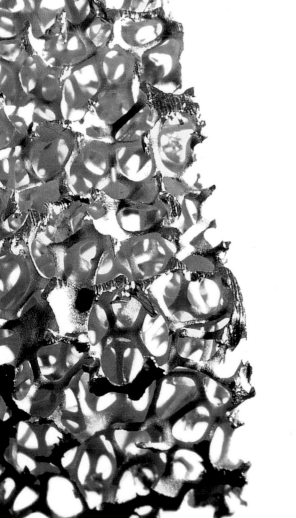

Duocel® aluminum
6101 alloy 10 PPI metal
foam sample
Manufacturer: Materials
and Aerospace Corp.

Metal foam

There are some materials that need no introduction to motivate designers, like sheets of translucent polypropylene, for example. Coveted samples of these inspirational materials are often kept close at hand by designers who bide their time, waiting for just the right commission in order to fully exploit their appealing qualities. These are the kind of semi-formed materials that designers often discover have been used in industrial applications for years.

This lightweight aluminum alloy foam combines qualities you would normally find in a natural form using metallic alloys. These metals are highly valued for their mechanical properties: the large surface area, their high strength-to-weight ratio, and so on. Within these high-performance materials lies a network of air pockets: an interconnecting, 3D mesh that is as intriguing as a natural sponge or a piece of coral.

Dimensions	**6–8 percent density; 90mm x 40mm**
Key Features	**Stiff**
	High strength-to-weight ratio for superior performance
	Less than 10 percent of the weight of solid aluminum
	Can be cut, turned, milled, and ground
	Can accept a range of finishes
More	**www.ergaerospace.com**
Typical Applications	**Heat sinks for electronic components, aircraft wing structures, energy absorbers for car fenders, flow straightness in wind tunnels, structures for high-strength panels, heat shields for aircraft exhausts, jet engine silencers, energy absorption for blast shock-waves, and structural elements for satellites.**

Paper-thin

This is steel that you can fold like paper, bend, join, print, and color. You can create, enhance, experiment, and, most of all, surprise with this innovative new material by Corus Packaging Plus.

Proflex is a new ultra-thin steel that can be used for new and innovative applications. It means that designers can create packaging that is structurally different due to its formable properties. Proflex is an unconventional ultra-thin steel with properties that make it unique and environmentally friendly. It is visually striking due to its excellent capacity to hold high-definition print.

Proflex is available in a variety of colors due to the different polymer coatings that can be used. This, combined with the range of grades available—from hard to soft—makes Proflex conducive to all shaping and decorative techniques such as embossing, gluing, heat sealing, bending etc., to create innovative packaging designs.

Dimensions	**750–950 mm wide; 80–120 microns thick**
Key Features	**Ultra-thin**
	Flexible
	Ductile
	Formable
	Tactile
	Available in a variety of colors and grades
	100 percent recyclable
More	**www.corusspace.com**
Typical Applications	**The main areas of design that currently exploit this material are within the packaging industry. Corus Packaging Plus encourages designers to explore its potential in packaging and other new applications.**

Samples of ultra-thin
polymer-coated material
by film application
or direct extrusion
**Manufacturer: Corus
Packaging Plus**

Dimensions	5,200mm long x 1,100mm wide sheet
Key Features	Ductile
	Easily forms alloys
	High strength-to-weight ratio
	Excellent corrosion-resistance
	Good heat and electricity conductor
	Recyclable
More	www.ingo-maurer.com
Typical Applications	Vehicle construction, aircraft parts, kitchen utensils, packaging, and furniture. Aluminum is also used for strengthening large structures, including the Statue of Eros in London and the top of the Chrysler building in New York.

Poetry of materials

Feathers, LEDs, broken crockery, and draped fabrics are all part of Ingo Maurer's palette of materials and references. There are few designers who choose to work predominantly in one typology, but Ingo Maurer has created a niche of poetic lighting experiences throughout his career. His exploration of and experimentation with material and lighting takes our understanding and definition of this area of design to higher planes. He uses light in the same way as an artist uses sculpture to explore form and space.

Paragaudi was a site-specific project designed for a private house in Len, Casa Botines, Spain, which was originally designed by the architect Antonio Gaudí. Maurer used gold-plated aluminum in this design to create a hanging cloud of precious metal, which appears to drift between the floor and the ceiling. Like a length of giant gold ribbon, the piece exploits the lightweight quality of aluminum, and the precious quality of gold.

**Paragaudi Light
Designer: Ingo Maurer**

Lightweight

Dimensions	**2,007mm x 1,438mm x 5,034mm**
Key Features	**High strength-to-weight ratio**
	Forms alloys easily
	Excellent corrosion-resistance
	Excellent heat and electricity conductor
	Ductile
	Recyclable
More	**www.audi.com**
	www.world-aluminum.org
Typical Applications	**Vehicle construction, aircraft parts, kitchen utensils, packaging, furniture, and strengthening large structures.**

Audi A8
Designer: Audi

Aluminum is a relatively recent addition to the world of metals. Audi have embraced this high-tech, lightweight material with its incredible mechanical properties, and made it a major feature of their brand—testament to their commitment to developing and using advanced engineering and materials.

Audi's development of lightweight vehicles goes back to the beginning of the twentieth century when they produced the NSU 8/24 car with its aluminum body. More recently the A2 and A8 models have exploited the material to an even greater degree—the A2 was the first volume-built vehicle with an all-aluminum body. This versatile metal has become so integral to Audi's business that in 1994 they inaugurated the Audi Aluminum Center in Neckarsulm, Germany, where aluminum and associated technologies are promoted and developed.

The A8 model offers a substantial weight reduction compared with similar cars. The space frame weighs only 215kg, almost half the weight of an equivalent frame in steel.

New function

Spectacle case
Manufacturer: Lindberg

Lindberg has designed a spectacle case to match its unique and simple spectacle frames. The case, like the frames, is inspired by the Danish/Scandinavian design traditions of simplicity, material minimalism, and functionality. The concept for this unique design is based on the fundamental idea of optimizing the choice of materials and design in relation to functional requirements.

The case is made from one thin sheet of brushed stainless steel. It is an example of the optimum application of sheet steel and its inherent properties of strength and flexibility. The steel sheet has been shaped with the utmost accuracy to create the closing mechanism which functions perfectly without the use of hinges, screws, soldering, or other external features, just like the frames. The case is functional as well as robust—ideal for contemporary, lightweight spectacles.

Dimensions	**66mm x 153mm; 63mm x 143mm**
Key Features	**Noncorrosive**
	Capable of an outstanding surface finish
	Excellent toughness
	Can be formed using a variety of processes
More	**www.lindberg.com**
Typical Applications	**Stainless steel has revolutionized industry. Generally used where there is the risk of corrosion and a need for heat-resistance, including kitchen equipment, tableware, architectural applications, engine components, fasteners, and tools and dies for production.**

Ron Arad has developed a collection of designs based on the challenge he sets himself of finding novel product typologies based on new manufacturing techniques. His body of work is filled with examples of furniture and products that are the result of applying new methods, often borrowed from other industries.

"I wanted to use the Superform process for furniture and had to wait a while until a suitable project came up; the first was a chair. Another opportunity arose when I was commissioned to do a sculpture in Milan, and eventually I was able to transfer the shapes we had made into plastic."

The Tom-Vac chair started life as a product made using the Superform aluminum process. This process exploits thin aluminum alloys up to a maximum thickness of 10mm and offers the potential to create strong, lightweight shapes that would normally only be realized in plastic.

Soft metal

Dimensions	690mm wide x 550mm deep
Key Features	Complex forms can be created in a single component
	A range of thicknesses can be used
	Subtle details and forms can be created
	No spring-back issues
	A range of aluminum alloys can be used
More	www.ronarad.com
	www.superform-aluminium.com
Typical Applications	Superform components can be formed into many alloys for use in a range of industries including aerospace, transport, and furniture.

Tom-Vac superformed, mirror-polished, aluminum stacking chair with stainless steel frame
Designer: Ron Arad
Manufacturer: Superform Aluminum

Tongue doodles

Ordering this jewelry by mail gives everyone a chance to become a designer. This unique jewelry design and production method honors the 3D tongue doodle imprinted on individual sticks of chewing gum. Each simple stick of gum is a potential piece of jewelry just waiting to be brought to life by its chewer.

How to make your own brooch:
• Remove the chewing gum from the box and find a comfortable place, i.e. the bathtub, a nature spot, a subway etc. Then start chewing.
• Take your time. Look on the back of the package for inspiration if needed. Create some different shapes. Once you have settled on your favorite design, send it back to Ted Noten in the original box (mailing is included in the cost).
• Noten will then make a mold of your chewed gum and cast it in silver. After soldering a pin onto the back and plating it in 24 carat gold, he'll send you your finished piece.

Chew Your Own
Brooch jewelry
Manufacturer: Ted Noten

Dimensions	**70mm x 24mm**
Key Features	**Unique approach to designer/maker relationship**
	Any shape is possible
	Can be applied to a range of metals
More	**www.tednoten.com**
Typical Applications	**Casting is used for forming virtually any shape. Applications other than jewelry include decorative figurines, statues, tableware, furniture, accessories, and industrial components.**

Metallic skin

Key Features	**Decorative**
	Acts as a light barrier
	Printable and reflective
	Heat insulator and electrical conductor
More	**www.isseymiyake.com**
	www.schlenk.de
	www.seppleaf.com
	www.gilders-warehouse.co.uk
Typical Applications	**Metal leaves are used in a range of applications including candy wrappers, packaging for medicine and food, stamping foils, cable wrap insulation, and heat reflection.**

Issey Miyake stands out as one of the most pioneering fashion designers of recent times. He has provided us with an ongoing spectacular feast of new fabrics and garments, often with incredible properties. He continues to break ground—his Starburst Collection is a range of clothes that are encased in metal. Paper-thin foils are heat-pressed onto the clothes, producing flat, foil-wrapped garments. When the garment is stretched over the body, the foil is torn open, creating a shredded-foil effect.

Glove from the
Starburst Collection
Designer: Issey Miyake

Surface code

In 1999, furniture designer Tom Longhurst and graphic designer Simon Procter combined their disciplines to create their debut product. The market had not yet seen a high-end sculptural tile in metal. They experimented with various metals to create different textures and forms, using Morse Code as their theme. They eventually settled on aluminum as it met most of their requirements for production.

The manufacturing process of sand-casting meant that they could meet both small and large production runs, and no structural fixings were needed because of its lightness. Most importantly the finished tiles had a hand sculpted aesthetic. The Morse tiles were originally designed for prestige architectural commissions but their exposure has extended well beyond this niche market to more mainstream environments such as kitchens and nightclubs.

Morse aluminum tiles
Designers: Tom Longhurst
and Simon Procter

Dimensions	**315mm x 315mm x 6mm; 9 tiles make 1,000mm²**
Key Features	**Durable in both interior and exterior environments**
	Handmade appearance
	Lightweight
	Endless possibilities for design layouts
	Messages can be written in code
	Gluing possible (no fixings)
	Can be sold as a single art piece or as signage
Typical Applications	**High-end hotel receptions, bars, nightclubs, restaurants, airline lounges, and large show rooms. These tiles have also been used as a background for photo shoots including for a Levi's clothing range.**

Metallic tissue

Textile technology is an astonishing area for the number of industries it extends into, encompassing virtually all areas of engineering and design, from the wearable to the habitable. It is not just the arenas in which they are used but the fact that textiles can incorporate natural and synthetic fibers made from glass, ceramics, and metals. These advanced materials can be molded and formed to create 3D pieces. Even when their purpose is purely decorative, the industry is revolutionizing the way textiles are perceived.

Charisma is the brand name of a range of intriguing sheets of metal with a structure that consists of thousands of long, thin aluminum fibers compressed together in a polyester matrix and produced in a vacuum to form a totally flat sheet. This metallic material, which is available in four finishes was originally designed for window blinds. The pattern comes from the swirl of fibers formed on the sheet which is highly crease-resistant and feels more like paper than fabric. This material is crying out for designers to find new areas in which to use it.

Dimensions	2,100mm x 40,000mm rolls
Key Features	Unique decorative potential
	Resin can be added to form a laminate
	Flat
More	www.jm-textile.com
Typical Applications	The main application for these textiles has so far been in window blinds. They have also been used as part of moldings to produce decorative surfaces.

Charisma metallic textiles

Decorative corrosion

One of the most interesting qualities of a piece of metal is its living surface. Like wood, metals are transformed by nature, creating patterns that remind us of the earth that they come from. Corrosion is a fascinating aspect of their behavior, which can transform shiny surfaces into unique, decorative patterns and textures. In a controlled environment, this corrosive process can be exploited to create beautiful ornamentation.

Architect Jean Nouvel designs buildings that are sympathetic to their surroundings. So it follows that a steel building which is surrounded by water should make some reference to the corrosion that takes place when these two natural elements come together.

Floating on Lake Morat in Switzerland, this cube of 4,000 tonnes of rusty steel was designed by Nouvel for the Swiss Expo 2002. Resting on a platform of reinforced concrete, and rising some 98 ½ feet (30m) above the water, the rusty box exploits the transitional effect nature has on steel.

Dimensions	27,600m² floor area
Key Features	Tough
	Easy to form
	Strong
	Relatively inexpensive
	Needs little energy to recycle
More	www.jeannouvel.fr
Typical Applications	Construction, shipping, production tooling, bridges, cars, railways, furniture, household goods, and architecture.

Monolith
Designer: Jean Nouvel
and GIMM Architekten
Client: Swiss Expo 2002

Sun protection

The increasing use of large sheets of glass within architecture gives the obvious benefit of natural light, but also allows too much sun and heat into buildings. This award-winning transparent sunshade system is made of roll-formed, hollow sections of stainless steel, and was developed by Clauss Markisen and Projekt GmbH, with Tilmann Kuhn, who focused on the shape of the steel section.

The roll-up sunshade transfers very little energy into buildings and can withstand winds of up to 55 km/h. The height of one hollow section is 4mm, and the gaps between the sections amount to 20 percent of the total area of the blind, providing good visibility as well as sun protection. The optimized shape of the sections of stainless steel provide shade from direct sunlight, even when the sun is more than 20 degrees above the horizon, which reduces air-conditioning costs considerably.

"Maximizing energy efficiency and daylight should be standard when planning and designing buildings. The more daylight and solar energy are utilized in a building, the more important it is to balance the supply of daylight, glare protection, and overheating protection; these three aspects are inseparable," says Kuhn.

Dimensions	Each section 4mm high
Key Features	High sun-protection
	High visibility
	Energy efficient
	Can withstand winds of up to 55km/h
More	www.clauss-markisen.de
	www.ise.fhg.de
Typical Applications	Sun protection.

Sunshade
Designer: Clauss
Markisen Projekt GmbH
and Fraunhofer ISE
Trade mark: senn_®

Metallic tapestries

**Architectural metal
screens
Manufacturer: Gebr
Kufferath AG**

Dimensions	**8,000mm maximum width; unlimited length**
Key Features	**Decorative**
	Wide range of woven styles
	Nonflammable
	Highly durable
	Easy to clean
	Graffiti deterrent
	Fireproof
	Corrosion-resistant
More	**www.creativeweave.com**
Typical Applications	**To date, these products have been used mainly for architectural and interior purposes including building facades, wall partitions, exhibition stands, screens, ceilings, handrail barriers, wire weaving mills, and reflective surfaces.**

These metallic, architectural fabrics can be used to create beautiful, sweeping drapes and tapestries. There are endless optical and functional possibilities within interior and exterior applications for these revolutionary materials. Metallic fabrics have translucent, delicate surfaces that can act as screens to hide pipes, sprinkler systems, acoustic insulation, and so on without hindering their function.

The metallic sheets are an interesting combination of stainless steel mesh, chains, and woven structures, providing a durable, nonflammable alternative to traditional textiles. On a large scale, the palette of patterns and textures can be exploited to dramatically change the surface of a building. As large, textured sheets, they are transformed into metal curtains, carpets, and seductive backdrops due to their ability to reflect so much light.

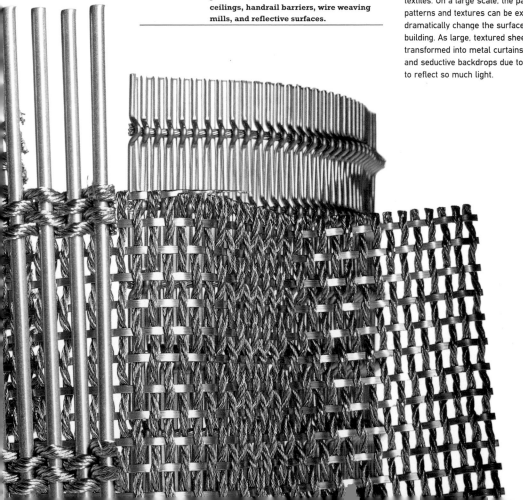

142

Humanufacturing

Once separated from any additives, many metals can be reused and recycled in countless forms. Designer Boris Bally not only embraces metals for their sustainable qualities, he also ensures that their former life is respected in the new forms that he creates. He calls the process of making these aluminum chairs "humanufacturing," as they are handmade from collected scrap, and require only light equipment to form.

Ingredients
- 99 percent recycled metals
- Virgin metals
- Steel fasteners
- Aluminum tubes

Method
- Bally selects scrap signs for their imagery, condition, material, thickness, and surface.
- Blanks are traced with a template and cut to size with a metal bandsaw.
- The parts are shaped using a small brake press. Holes are drilled and edges deburred. The tongue-and-groove pattern in the seats is shaped with a jigsaw and jeweler's files.
- Screws are inserted and the parts aligned. The feet are cut from tube and turned on a small lathe. Champagne corks are slotted in and the tubes are fixed to the legs.
- The chairs are taken apart and each component is scrubbed by hand.
- Parts are inspected and stamped.
- Final deburring, then spray and seal.
- Parts are reassembled, inspected for fit, then taken apart and packed in a recyclable cardboard box ready for shipping.

New Transit chairs
Designer: Boris Bally

Dimensions	200mm high x 406mm wide x 533mm deep
Key Features	Recycled waste material
	Low-tech production
	Handmade
More	www.borisbally.com
	www.snagmetalsmith.org
Typical Applications	Aluminum is recycled in many forms, large amounts of which are melted and reformed.

Durable

Dimensions	225mm x 104mm x 129mm; 1mm thick
Key Features	**Corrosion-resistant**
	Highly durable
	Infinite range of colors
	Can be used on a range of materials
More	**www.bludot.com**
	www.powdercoating.org
Typical Applications	**Powder coating is used in many diverse areas, from the automotive industry, where it is used for car body panels, to washing machines, refrigerators, bicycles, and filing cabinets.**

**Desktop CD holder
Designers: John Christakos,
Charles Lazor and Maurice
Blanks at Blu Dot
Client: Blu Dot**

Principally driven by the desire to protect, metal finishes offer a huge range of surface designs. These coatings provide opportunities to alter the visual and tactile qualities of the base materials. The glassy, hard, enamelled finish of powder coatings combines raw, industrial function with a brutally effective, protective layer. Powder coating uses an electrically-charged pigment together with resin powder. Similar to the build-up of static electricity on plastic combs, the powder is attracted to the metal, building up an even coating. Blu Dot use this hard coating to enhance many of their domestic accessories.

The pleasure of self-assembly with this Blu Dot range of products is derived from the ability of the metals to bend easily and hold their shape. Carefully measured slots reduce the amount of material on the fold lines, allowing the metal to bend with the correct degree of resistance, while holding its final shape. From flat sheet to 3D product in minutes, this is flatpack in its simplest form.

The surface of an object acts as a boundary between that object and the atmosphere. This barrier can be natural or it can be created to act as a decorative or a protective coating. Some metal alloys have an invisible, self-healing coating, and there a few that are used to form new coatings on different materials.

Electroplating is the process of applying a metal to the surface of another material to form a coating by means of electrolysis. It involves two main elements: a cathode and an anode in an electrolyte solution. The cathode is the object to be plated and the anode is the metalizing coating. A direct current moves metal ions from the anode to the cathode. Virtually anything can be electroplated. These fake surfaces offer materials new sensory qualities, challenging preconceptions and conventions, as with this gold, electrically-conductive wood.

The surface

Dimensions	**150mm²**
Key Features	**Enhances surface decoration**
	Improves corrosion-resistance
	Improves electrical conductivity
	Protects materials from electromagnetic and radio frequency radiation
More	**www.namf.org**
	www.finishing.com
	www.sea.org.uk
	www.bjsco.com
	www.aesf.org
Typical Applications	**Electroplating is mainly used to coat metals. This can take the form of silver-plated cutlery, jewelry, electrical and engineering components, and tableware. Also used for decorative purposes.**

Gold electroplated wood from the Shri Swaminarayan Mandir temple, London

Designer Afroditi Krassa says of her innovative Floating Light: "Metallic plastic was used for this project for functional reasons. Mylar® is the lightest material that will hold helium for a long time. There are other materials that are used for balloons, like latex or fabrics coated with polyurethane, but these are too heavy and would have required a much larger balloon diameter just to lift the material.

"One option was to have the light on the inside of the balloon but this brought other problems. Mylar® comes in a white finish for people to print over, but I decided to use the reflective nature of this metallic surface as a reflector for the light.

"The nylon net holds the balloon and the light source, which is a cluster of 91 LED lights. The balloon acts as a reflector and the whole thing is anchored by this base which holds all the electronic gear and extra cable, which can be used to adjust the height of the light."

Light reflector

Dimensions	1,000mm tall x 1,000mm diameter
Key Features	Gas barrier
	Light barrier and reflector
	Allows for printing
	Good heat insulator
	Electrical conductor
More	www.afroditi.com
	www.dupontteijinfilms.com
Typical Applications	Metal is used as a coating on plastics to fulfill many functions from foils in food packaging to hot air balloons. Mylar® allows for a unique combination of plastics and metals in products such as magnetic audio and video tape, capacitor dielectrics, packaging, cable wrap insulation tape, and drumheads. It is also used as a substrate for printing graphics.

Floating Light
Designer: Afroditi Krassa
Manufacturer: Afroditi Krassa

Growing a surface

An anodized finish is an aluminum oxide protective skin, which is grown from the aluminum by immersing it in an acid-electrolyte bath and passing an electrical current through it, toughening and significantly thickening its natural oxide coating. There are various forms of anodizing which all produce different finishes, including chromic anodizing, sulphuric anodizing, and hard anodizing. Sulphuric anodizing offers the greatest color variety.

Although anodizing has helped to make aluminum one of the most widely used materials within consumer markets and industry, it is often thought of as a surface finish only for aluminum. However, it is applied to other metals including magnesium, titanium, zirconium, and zinc.

Dimensions	**Sizes from 81mm to 424mm long**
Key Features	**Unique decorative surface**
	Durable
	Available in a range of colors
	Corrosion-resistant
More	**www.maglite.com**
	www.anodizing.org
Typical Applications	**Anodizing finishes can be found on engineering components, exteriors of buildings, various interior design applications, domestic appliances, furniture, pens, and exterior panels for aerospace vehicles.**

Mini Maglite® flashlight
Designer: Anthony Maglica
Manufacturer: Mag Instruments, Inc.

Hardwearing protection

We are drawn to shiny, reflective surfaces of all kinds, including chrome finishes which reflect so perfectly. Chrome plating has helped to elevate some products to iconic status, classic cars being the most obvious example. There are three types of chrome plating, which are referred to by various names but can be commonly classified as decorative plating, hard chromium plating, and black chrome plating. The thickness of the chromium layer varies depending on the type. The nature of this kind of plating means that whatever the existing surface of the material, the coating will pick it up, so when plating a matte surface you are left with a matte chrome finish.

When considering chrome plating, it is very important to be aware of the hazards of the process. In recent years, there has been a strong movement away from the traditional hexavalent decorative chromium baths, which are extremely carcinogenic, to the newer trivalent chromium baths, which are considered to be less toxic.

Dimensions	**420mm high; 200mm diameter of base**
Key Features	**Decorative**
	Outstanding corrosion-resistance
	Low coefficient of friction
	Hard
More	**www.sea.org.uk**
	www.namf.org
	www.finishing.com
Typical Applications	**Decorative chrome plating is used for kitchenware, tableware, packaging, electronic products, and vehicle components, including door handles and bumpers. Hard chrome plating is used for more industrial applications, including rams on JCBs, components for jet engines, plastic moldings, and shock absorbers. Black chrome plating is used for decoration on musical instruments and solar applications.**

Chrome-based portable fan

Engineering detail

This amplifier is part of a range of high-end audiophile products. It is an example of a functional engineering finish often used in watches (the milled surface retains as much lubricant on the moving parts for as long as possible) that has been decoratively applied to a consumer product. The Jeff Rowland Design Group used this finish for their amplifiers to suggest a technologically advanced product.

The faceplate is milled from 0.75mm 6061 aircraft aluminum stock and is machined with a 0.001mm deep fly-cut pattern on a special machine, with a unique diamond-tipped bit. Once the metal is diamond cut, the raw metal is covered with a fine, clear coat to prevent the finish from dulling or oxidizing. No anodizing is used on the faceplates. The logo is machined into the faceplate and then filled in by hand with gloss black lacquer. Each faceplate is kept in its own metal container to protect the finish until needed.

Dimensions	469mm deep x 254mm high x 368mm wide
Key Features	High tolerance
	Retains lubrication
More	www.jeffrowland.com
Typical Applications	This surface is typically used in engineering applications to retaining oil on a finish. It can also be the by-product of milling a surface to create a tolerant, flat surface.

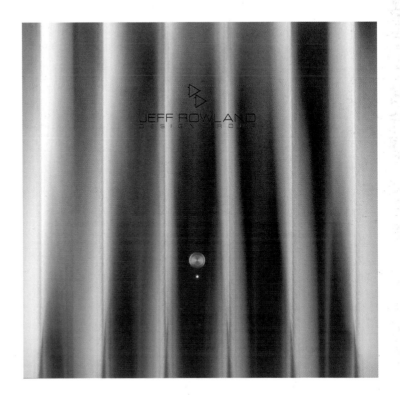

**Model 302 stereo
power amplifier
Designer: Jeff Rowland
and Vertec Tool
Manufacturer: Jeff
Rowland Design Group**

155 Plastic

Plastic money

Mylar® and Melinex® are two of the most common polyester films. They can be used for a vast range of applications from video and printed circuit boards to laminating ripstop nylon for entrepeneur Richard Branson to use on his hot air balloons. For the purpose of the balloons, 12-micron-thick Melinex® was able to remain flexible at temperatures of -94°F(-70°C) while also withstanding the heat from the burners. In the food packaging industry it is used as a lid for ready meals which are kept in freezers and are immediately put in an oven, proving that it is dimensionally stable. It can also take printing very well, another advantage for its use in packaging. Melinex® as a printed film for reprographics springs back to a flat sheet even when tightly rolled up and is heat- and chemical- resistant.

Dimensions	**Available from 12–350 microns**
Production	**Printed extruded sheet**
Key Features	**Good temperature- and chemical-resistance**
	Good optical clarity
	Excellent print capabilities
	Recyclable
	Rigid
	Excellent strength compared to cellulose acetate film
	Good dimensional stability
	Nontoxic
More	**www.dupontteijinfilms.com**
Typical Applications	**Food wrapping, credit cards, labels, dart fins, substrate for printed circuit boards, x-ray films, motor insulation, wind surfing sails, lids on yogurt pots, and protective window film.**

Glassy smooth

To deliver eight gallons of beer you would need 27lb of glass bottles or 8lb of steel. With polyethylene terephthalate (PET) you only need 5lb. The use of plastic as a replacement for glass means you can take your beer into places that usually prohibit anything in glass.

PET is commonly used for food and soft drinks packaging. However, due to beer being more oxygen and carbon dioxide sensitive, PET was not suitable. Altogether there are five layers in each bottle; sandwiched between three layers of PET are two layers of oxygen scavengers which prevent oxygen getting in or out. Miller Brewing Company who launched its first plastic bottle in 2000, claim it keeps beer cooler longer than aluminum cans and as long as glass. It can also be resealed and is unbreakable.

Dimensions	**Height 210mm; diameter 70mm**
Production	**Injection blow molded**
Key Features	**Recyclable (PET is one of the most recycled plastic resins)**
	Excellent resistance to chemicals
	Excellent dimensional stability
	Tough and durable
	Excellent surface finish
	Good impact strength
More	**www.dsm.com**
Typical Applications	**Food packaging, electrical products, and soft drinks bottles.**

Miller beer bottle
Designer: Continental PET
Technologies
Client: Miller Brewing
Company

The growing awareness of waste management has produced many innovative ways of recycling waste into new products and materials. Much of our waste is packaging related. After use it is thrown into our trashcans and transported to expensive landfill sites or incinerators.

Smile Plastics is one of many companies across the world committed to sourcing and developing innovative ideas and markets for recycled materials, concentrating on transforming plastics into multicolored sheets. What separates these sheets from other post-waste products are the layers of disgarded shampoo bottles, rain boots, and yogurt pots, which can be seen in the surface. This process produces sheets of plastic material, which unlike other plastic sheets are not all identical. The original waste is collected, sorted, flaked, and thoroughly washed to remove any remaining contaminants. Looking like multicolored cornflakes, the pieces are then compressed into sheets by a process of heat and pressure, which retains the colors of the original bottles. These sheets can be sawn, drilled, routed, and planed using conventional workshop tools. The surface requires no treatment, not even a sealant. Each product has a unique tactile feel from waxy to rubbery.

Dimensions	2,000mm x 1,000mm; various thicknesses
Key Features	Distinct visual appearance
	Easy to process
	No tooling investment
	Available in a range of thicknesses
More	www.smile-plastics.co.uk
Typical Applications	Furniture, interiors, and work surfaces.

Trash!

Designer: Colin Willamson
Client: Smile Plastics

Celebrity status

Jumo Desk Lamp

Bakelite was declared "the material of a thousand uses," when it was discovered in the first part of the twentieth century. The promotion of Bakelite went hand in hand with the emergence of the new profession of industrial designers. Raymond Loewy was often seen in Bakelite advertisements singing the praises of the new plastic material. It was one of the first plastics that gave designers freedom to create new aesthetics for products.

The name Bakelite is also the name of a company that produces phenolics and other materials. Phenolic resin does not work well with the addition of colors which is why phenolics are generally dark colors. Today phenolics are largely used as binders or adhesives in the production of board material and laminates. As a molding compound it can easily be reinforced by fillers and fibers that offer strength and prevent the product being too brittle. One of its few modern day uses is as handles for cookware.

Key Features	Good heat- and flame-resistance
	High impact-resistance
	Low-cost material
	Excellent dimensional stability
	Nontoxic
	Good hardness and scratch-resistance
	Outstanding electrical insulation
	Best suited to dark colors
	Brittle if molded in thin wall thickness
	Hard as a solid component
More	www.bakelite.ag
Typical Applications	Brake linings, oasis foam support for flowers, binding for laminated wood panels, saucepan handles, and door handles.

Color is not often the main priority in a designer's specification. It tends to fall some way behind form and material on the sketch sheet, and often appears as the dressing once the other details are in order. However, the importance of color in design should never be understated.

Color is one of the first things we notice, consciously or unconsciously, when we look at an object. It is also one of the main driving forces behind trends, and can provide the revamping of a product's identity without the need to completely retool the product itself.

Through the addition of a masterbatch, designers have a limitless range of possibilities for color and decoration. Masterbatches are additives to any number of molded plastic products that serve to enhance performance and/or add color and detail.

Snap was created as an alternative to the plastic color samples that are traditionally sent out to designers. The object, consisting of 60 identical components that show the 18 colors, was created by Tom Dixon for Gabriel-Chemie, one of Europe's leading masterbatch producers, to highlight the potential for color in the molding of plastics.

Exploring color's full potential

Dimensions	360mm diameter
Key Features	Decoration is embedded into the surface, which eliminates the possibility of colors being worn or scratched off
	Not limited to color; can also be extended to other effects or additional properties
More	www.tomdixon.net
	www.gabriel-chemie.com
Typical Applications	Masterbatches are added to any number of molded plastic products to enhance performance and add color. Various masterbatches include anti-microbial additives to enhance strength and durability, wear-resistance, environmental-resistance, plasticizers to soften plastics, and a range of decorative effects.

Key Features	**Exceptional flexibility when sandwiched**
	Excellent energy absorption
	Cost-effective
	Low cost, high production rates
	Recyclable
More	**www.cellbond.net**
Typical Applications	**This structural panel has uses in aerospace, architectural, marine, and automotive industries. It can be used for ceiling and roof panels in the rail and automotive industry, in the manufacture of hoods and fenders in cars, as decorative panels in the retail and home environments, for raised floors, interior and exterior cladding, and for room dividers. It can also be used for impact protection in transport, including the front wings of vehicles, and in exhibition stands and decorative panels.**

Material becomes surface

There is always great innovation based on making the most from as little as possible. Many lightweight but strong panel products are built on the idea of trapping air inside a rigid geometry or the sandwiching of different materials.

PressLoad, made by Cellbond Composites, however, uses a clever surface design to create a valuable combination of strength, energy absorption, and lightness.

Based on the same principle as an egg box, this is a semi-formed material, born out of technical innovation and designed for a robust engineering use. It also happens to be a fascinating material visually. Originally developed as a lightweight energy absorber to compete with honeycomb and other panel products, PressLoad is more of an innovation as a surface than as a material.

There is a range of different geometries and materials according to application. Beyond thermoset and thermoformed plastics, which include polypropylene and polycarbonate, the principle of this surface can also be used in aluminum alloys. Although the standard form is a sheet, PressLoad can also be formed into curves, where it performs well as an impact absorber.

Total clarity

Dimensions	**142mm x 124mm**
Key Features	**High clarity**
	Cost-effective
	Ability to incorporate live hinges
	Widely available
	Low density
	Good chemical-resistance
	Good strength and rigidity
	Recyclable
More	**www.clearpp.com**
	www.milliken.com
Typical Applications	**There are numerous industries where clear polypropylene has applications. Some popular applications are in food and nonfood packaging, centrifugal tubes, disposable syringes for the medical industry, and blow-molded bottles.**

The introduction of plastics to industrial production sparked a revolution in the nature of the products that could be designed and produced. Of possibly equal significance was the point when the new super-morphing substance could be made transparent. This opened up the world of plastic to such an extent that it is now virtually synonymous with transparency.

When polypropylene (PP) was introduced, it ushered in a new area of possibilities for plastic products, including live hinges, cost-effectiveness, and toughness. What it lacked was the ability to be completely transparent, having a slight milky haze. When polypropylene is seen alone, this milkiness is not very evident, but when viewed next to a piece of PET (polyethylene terephthalate), it is obvious which one is transparent.

Milliken has a rich history of technical innovation, and since the early 1980s it has been developing clarifying agents to overcome this problem with PP. Its latest generation of clear polypropylene should help it compete more with the likes of crystal-clear PET.

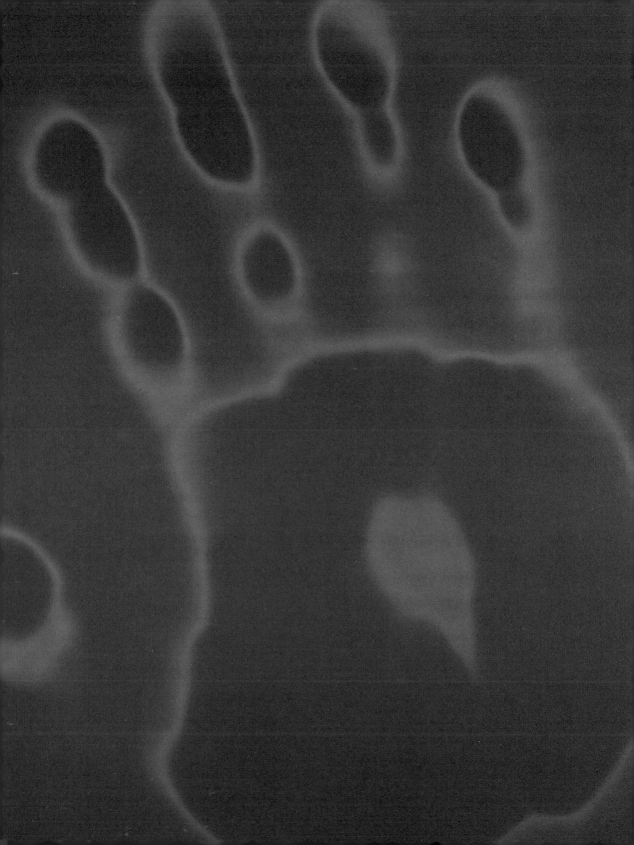

Invisible made visible

The interesting aspect of any type of thermochromic technology is that it makes visible that which is inherently invisible. It can take the warmth from your hand, for example, and convert it into a series of colors, thereby providing a new way of seeing our environment.

This type of color-changing technology can take various forms. Liquid-crystal thermochromics, for example, are based on the coding of different temperatures into a series of colors. This is the technology behind forehead thermometers, where the change in temperature is reflected by a different color.

ChromaZone is unique in the fact that it can supply anything from the initial powder and ink to a semi-finished thermochromic sheet or a finished thermometer. One particularly interesting product that the company produces is a heat-sensing ink in the form of a crayon.

ChromaZone is now looking at new applications for the products. The company has worked with a number of designers, including a fashion designer who has incorporated the technology into textiles.

Key Features	Can be used in a variety of forms
	Reversible or nonreversible
	Can be printed or molded
	High visual appeal
	Good safety potential
	Fun
More	www.chromazone.co.uk
Typical Applications	Thermochromics can be used in sheet form, printable form, and as a masterbatch additive to a molded product. Thermochromics are found in everything from children's products for testing the temperature of food and drink to industrial safety signage. They are also used in promotional products, sunglasses, packaging for batteries, novelty products, mood rings, and food packaging.

Unrippable

Welcome to the most exciting envelope material ever: a plastic that can be printed, glued, sewn, and, when you have finished with it, can be recycled and converted to car parts, underground cables, and blown film!

Tyvek® is an HDPE (high-density polyethylene fiber)—a plastic that thinks it's a paper. Tyvek® is one of the most well-known brands. If you don't know this brand by name, you will know it by the waxy, paper-thin, plastic sheet that is used to make, among other things, virtually unrippable courier envelopes. The texture of the material is the result of the strands of polyethylene in its cross-linked structure. Aware of the product's potential in other markets, DuPont has also introduced a range of metallic colors.

TYVEK® is produced in three different types: 10, 14, and 16. The fibers in Type 10 style are bonded to form a tough, dense, opaque sheet. The dense packing of the fine, interconnected fibers produces a smooth surface, high opacity, and whiteness. The large number of bonds per unit area results in a stable and abrasion-resistant surface with a stiffness similar to paper. Fiber bonding of Types 14 and 16 is restricted to discreet points in the nonwoven sheet. This produces a high degree of fiber mobility, and gives the nonwoven sheet a fabric-like drape.

Tyvek® behaves like any paper product: you can write on it using pencil or pen, pencil marks can be rubbed out, it will not tear at folds, and it can be folded 20,000 times without wearing out. It even floats. When a hole is punched in it, this doesn't weaken the material. Tyvek® is printable by most common techniques (except hot laser and photocopying), and can be printed on most computer printers. With a material like this, who needs trees!

Key Features	Super-strong
	Lightweight
	Good liquid hold-out characteristics
	Strong and tear-resistant
	Weather-resistant
	Resists continuous folding and flexing
	Keeps properties across a wide range of temperatures
	Unaffected by most chemicals
	Nontoxic
	Chemically inert
	Conforms to International Maritime Dangerous Goods labeling code (also BS-5609)
	Approved for contact with foodstuffs and cosmetics
	Conforms to draft EC directives on packaging waste and German legislation on compatible labeling
More	www.duponttyvek.com
Typical Applications	Security envelopes, protective apparel, specialty packaging, roofing membranes, tags and labels, banners, maps, money, reinforcement, and kites.

Sample of DuPont Tyvek®

There is a seductiveness about a material that is solid and tough enough to withstand abuse but which has a water-like clarity. Clarity has been a preoccupation of design since the first clear plastics were developed. The molding of clarity offers our senses the chance to be cheated with solid, rigid enclosures containing electronics, packaging, and other objects.

Nas® is a brand of SMMA (styrene methylmethacrylate copolymer) from Nova Chemicals. It is marketed as a transparent alternative to SAN (styrene acrylonitrile), clear polystyrene, and acrylic, or for applications that require strong, stiff, clear components. It is also promoted as a lower-cost alternative to some of these plastics due to its ease of processing and lower density, which means more parts per kilogram of resin.

We take it for granted that transparent plastics are unexceptional, but before the invention of this relatively new material the only thing that was transparent was glass. Constricted by its fragility, risk when broken, and molding limitations, glass' impact on mass-production has been limited. The introduction of clear plastics heralded a quiet revolution in packaging, furniture, safety devices, medical goods, transport, and a wealth of other markets.

212 On Ice perfume bottle
Designer: Carolina Herrera NY
Manufacturer: Antonio Puig, S.A.

Clear alternative

Dimensions	130mm height x 62mm width x 62mm depth
Key Features	**Tough**
	Colors and decorates easily by print, hot stamp, and metalizing
	Sparkling clarity
	Lower density means more parts per kilogram of resin
	Low-cost processing
	Chemical-resistant
	Alcohol-resistant
	UL94 HB-approved
	FDA and USP Class VI-compliant
	Antistatic and indoor UV grades available
More	**www.novachem.com**
Typical Applications	**Tumblers, perfume bottle caps, handles for taps, medical devices, toys, waterfilter jugs, domestic cleaning appliances, and transparent rigid coat hangers.**

Power stools

Miura Bar Stool

This stool is a wonderful combination of material and product. Within its dynamic, stealth aesthetic lays an example of a structural use of plastic that is rarely seen.

There are chairs and stools that combine stable shapes and thin wall thickness to create strong structures, but they all seem to follow the same principles of form combined with established material. The Air chair by designer Jasper Morrison, for example, uses air injection molding to offer us a lightweight chair, but even that follows the same rules of form, with four legs and a backrest.

What Miura offers us though this shape is almost unprecedented as a plastic molding in a single piece, with its off-balance structure and cantilevered seat looking instead like something that should be cast from aluminum. Indeed, the manufacturers of this stool claim it is two-and-a-half times stronger than aluminum.

In its pure state polypropylene can be easily tailored to control its various features. For a commodity plastic it is reasonably stiff and rigid but, as with any plastic, the addition of reinforcement takes it to new levels of strength and stiffness.

Dimensions	**470mm x 400mm x 810mm**
Key Features	**Widely available**
	Low-density
	Good strength and rigidity
	Cost-effective
	Ability to incorporate live hinges
	Good chemical-resistance
	Recyclable
More	**www.plank.it**
	www.konstantin-grcic.com
Typical Applications	**Clear polypropylene has applications in food and nonfood packaging, centrifugal tubes and disposable syringes for the medical industry, blow-molded bottles, and food containers.**

Cloud Modules
Designers: Ronan & Erwan Bouroullec

The most banal applications of materials can disguise the fact that they have far richer applications than we might assume. Fitting snugly between the walls of the cardboard box and the protected product inside it is a humble, low-density, solid material that has unexplored potential: expanded polystyrene (EPS).

Polystyrene belongs to the styrene family of polymers, along with ABS (acrylonitrile butadiene styrene), SAN (styrene acrylonitrile), ASA (acrylic styrene acrylonitrile), and HIPS (high-impact polystyrene).

The production of polystyrene foam is based on tiny polystyrene beads that are expanded to 40 times their original size using a flow of steam and pentane. Steam is also used in

98 percent air

the final phase to inject the material into the mold. In comparison to EPP foam, polystyrene is less of a performance material, not having the range of densities, flexibility, and strength.

Although it is 98 percent air, polystyrene is often perceived as not being a friend of the environment. However, industry is keen to point out that polystyrene foam has never used CFCs (chlorofluorocarbons) or HCFCs (hydrochlorofluorocarbons) during production. The fact that the big and bulky bits of packaging are often not recycled but are left to accumulate enforces this negative perception. As a result, major steps have taken place in the last few years to provide recycling facilities. Once collected, the waste can be compacted and used to remold in its compacted form or ground down to form new products.

Dimensions	**1,050mm x 1,875mm x 400mm**
Key Features	**Cheap**
	Lightweight
	Durable
	Good insulation properties
	Shock absorbency
	Low hardness
	Insulating
	Recycled
	Easily branded
	Cushioning
More	**www.eps.co.uk**
	www.tuscarora.com
	www.kay-metzeler.com
	www.cappellini.it
	www.bouroullec.com
Typical Applications	**Typically found in disposable drinking cups for hot and cold drinks, expanded polystyrene has also been used on a much larger scale; for example, in housing in the Netherlands as a buoyant platform. A house in the UK has also been made entirely from expanded polystyrene. In horticultural applications, it is used to control temperature around root growth. In other forms, polystyrene foam is extruded and then thermoformed into trays and egg boxes.**

170

Plastic with a shelf life

Here's the idea. You are a busy person, with too many little jobs that fill your day. You want to rent a movie, but first you have to drive to the store to pick up the movie— and later, go back to return the disc. Time taking your DVD back is wasted time. Can you really be bothered?

But then you find out about Flexplay, a type of DVD that expires 48 hours after opening the package. No need to take the movie back; just let the information die. Unopened, the disc stays "fresh" in the package for about a year. Once exposed to oxygen, you have 48 hours to play the disc as many times as you want in any standard DVD player. After 48 hours, your time is up and the disc turns from bright red to black and is no longer playable. Just recycle the now-useless polycarbonate disc.

What is most interesting about this technology is not the fact that it might change the way we rent movies, because that is open to other electronic technologies, but that it raises the question: what if more products and plastics were like organic matter, and had shorter natural lifespans?

Dimensions	**120mm diameter**
Key Features	**Based on an existing polycarbonate substrate, the new key feature is that of data with a shelf life**
More	**www.flexplay.com**
	www.geplastics.com
Typical Applications	**The technology raises ethical questions about whether consumers will actually recycle the discs or just trash them. This type of technology has the potential to change the way we respond to products and affect the life cycles of plastic production and distribution.**

Flexplay ez-D™ 48-hour
no-return DVD
Manufacturer: Flexplay
Technologies, Inc

EdiZONE LC invents new technologies and develops them into products that are licensed to various markets. They have developed a core of three basic technologies, for which they have filed several patents, in the area of what can be described as supergels and foams. Within this range of technologies lies three fantastically soft gel-cushioning materials: Gelastic™, Intelli-Gel™, and Floam™.

Gelastic™ is a thermoplastic elastomeric copolymer gel, so it can be extruded, cast or injection molded. It can be formulated into a range of hardnesses and is extremely strong. Gelastic™ forms the bases for a second technology: Intelli-Gel™. This is a semiformed material that combines the intrinsic cushioning qualities of Gelastic™ into a cell structure. This exploits the effect of column buckling to allow objects to sink into the cushion without increasing the unit pressure of the object. Floam™, or Z-Flo™ as it is known in some markets, is the world's lightest nongas fluid. It is used as a filling inside a plastic bladder to distribute pressure evenly in applications such as hospital bedding to prevent bedsores.

Although generally used under a secondary skin and not exposed, these plastics are some of the most seductive materials you will find. They have a beautiful tinted translucency and the feel of a slightly sticky, semi-wet sponge. Behind this rich range of sensuous playfulness lies a selection of materials with serious applications. However, EdiZONE is keen to point out that no matter how exciting the potential for the materials appears, they are strictly for high-volume mass-production.

Key Features	Very stable
	Close to body temperature
	Does not alter properties with changes in temperature
	Super-strong
More	www.edizone.com
Typical Applications	These materials are used in a wide range of cushioning products. The principle behind the materials is that they distribute pressure over the whole object so that it is cushioned. Thus applications include surgical tourniquets, which are used to prevent damage to tissue while preventing excessive bleeding during surgery. Nike has used Floam™ under the name Nike Form in football and baseball cleats, snowboard boots, and skates. Other applications for Floam™ include orthopaedic support products and hospital bed mattresses for long-term care. Intelli-Gel™ is used as cushioning for the body, vibration dampening, and impact absorption. Finally, probably the most fun application is for a child's ultra-light, bouncy toy that uses the material as a molding compound.

Supergels

Sample of Intelli-Gel™
Manufacturer: Edizone LC

The world of shape memory materials is
a rich and fascinating one that includes
metals, plastics, fabrics, sheet materials,
and now foams. Unlike the metal and plastic
varieties, this foam does not use heat to
return to a "remembered" profile. Instead,
the material displays a much more modest
effect, similar to a super-viscous liquid that
allows for a slow release of an imprint that
has been pushed into its surface.

This range of high-memory or shock
absorbing foams (SAFs) is available in
several grades of softness and elasticity.
As with viscoelastic foams, they react to
gradual force with a viscous behavior,
and absorb shock-like forces with elastic
behavior. This behavior depends on
temperature, as the material becomes
more pliable when it is warm. This makes
it good for mattresses, for example, as
body warmth makes it more adaptable.

Shock absorbing foam is used in orthopedic
and medical mattresses and cushions to
prevent bedsores. It offers support similar
to gel or liquid cushions. The open-cell,
porous structure also allows the material
to breathe.

Key Features	**Good impact absorption**
	Has a small degree of memory
	Even distribution of pressure
More	**www.foampartner.com**
Typical Applications	**Orthopaedic bed mattresses, cushions, and shoes; sound absorption and dampening; impact absorption. Has also been used in flooring.**

Shock absorbing foam

Key Features	**Ability to expand**
	Relatively cheap
	Can be used without any big tooling on a craft scale
More	**www.industrialpolymers.com**
Typical Applications	**This material is described by Industrial Polymers as being like a "3D copy machine" and is promoted as a modeling material. Other applications could include toys or applications that use the reverse effect, exploiting the ability of the material to shrink when the water content dries out.**

Grow your own

Grow your own products with this flexible urethane resin! HydroSpan™ is a polyurethane-based product developed by Industrial Polymers. It relies on mixing together three main ingredients: hardener, resin, and plain water. As you would expect, the addition of water makes this stuff grow.

The process involves mixing the resin and hardener to make your component, which can be formed in a mold. In order to enlarge the cured part, it is left in a bath of water. The length of time required for the part to soak depends on its size and thickness. The manufacturers recommend that a part with a one-inch wall thickness will require about 14 days to expand to a maximum of 60 percent. The product can be removed from the water at any time, depending on how

much you want the piece to expand by. Once the part is fully soaked, the water is trapped inside the polymer matrix and the part feels completely dry. After several months, the material returns to its original size unless kept immersed in water. In terms of hardness, it feels like a stiff jelly, with a hardness of 45 Shore in its non-expanded state, and a slightly softer 35 Shore in its expanded state.

What this material begins to approach is the prospect of being able to grow products. At the moment, its main use is in model making, where it is used in scaling up small objects. It will be interesting to see whether it has applications for more consumer-led products.

Parton Swiss Army Knife
Designer: Victorinox
Manufacturer: Victorinox

In the 1930s, nylon (or polyamide, by its technical name) was one of the first engineering polymers to be discovered. Developed by DuPont, nylon has now become part of common language. Although existing in many forms, the properties across the family of resins vary due to the number of different formulations. However, nylon is characterized by its strength, toughness, and stiffness.

Strength, toughness, and stiffness

The Swiss army knife provides the perfect symbol for this tough plastic, and is perhaps the perfect match of product with material. Both product and material are icons and both are known for their ruggedness, with different versions and slight modifications and additions available. Two of the most widely used versions of nylon are nylon 6 and nylon 66. As a molding compound, it exhibits several superior qualities. When reinforced with glass, nylon becomes an even harder material. By itself, it is not one of the strongest engineering plastics, but has a natural waxy surface and the added advantage of being able to be cast, allowing for components several centimeters thick.

Dimensions	91mm x 10mm
Key Features	Slippery
	Good impact-resistance
	Tough
	Stiff
	Wear-resistant
	Able to achieve a high gloss
	Available clear or opaque
More	www.emsgrivory.com
Typical Applications	Well-known for being able to be drawn into silk-like fibers for clothing, nylon has a variety of uses and forms, including glass-reinforced molding compounds. Other applications include rope, engineering applications, and nutcrackers. Nylon is useful under the hood of cars, where its performance characteristics make them suitable for a variety of components. Low friction makes it useful for bearings, cams, and gears.

Dimensions	B-size chair: 1,067mm x 521mm x 432mm
Key Features	**Combines the moldability of plastics with the flexibility of rubber**
	Highly resistant to flex fatigue, chemicals, abrasion, and tearing
	Interior and exterior use
	Hytrel® can be blow, injection, and rotational molded, and extruded
	Breathable
More	**www.hermanmiller.com**
	www.quantum5280.com
	plastics.dupont.com
Typical Applications	**Hytrel® is a highly morphable material, lending itself to a range of forms that exploit its diverse properties. These include injection molded bed springs, office furniture, and the breathable layers on antiallergenic bedding.**

Design is having to become increasingly interdisciplinary, looking beyond conventional approaches to material conventions within traditional typologies. Hytrel® is a material that lends itself to such an approach. Not restricted to being just a molding compound, it can also be tailored to create fabrics and yarns. From DuPont, Hytrel® fibers have been licensed to textile company Quantum Group Inc. for use in a range of upholstery applications.

One of the most high-profile products to feature the fabric is the Aeron chair, manufactured by Herman Miller. This has become a modern-day icon for office chair design. Described by design critic Deyan Sudjic as the "stealth bomber of chairs," it uses a stack of engineering plastics, including Hytrel®. It has become a case study for how engineering plastics can be used for a host of structural applications.

As part of the brief to encompass pioneering ergonomics, the chair is designed to fit around the infinite range of human shapes and postures, taking into account the range of activities that take place during the day. The open-celled, breathable Hytrel® fabric that is used for the back and seat upholstery offers the design a sag-free, cushionable surface that replaces traditional foam.

Aeron chair
Designers: Bill Stumpf and
Don Chadwick
Manufacturer: Herman Miller

New cushioning

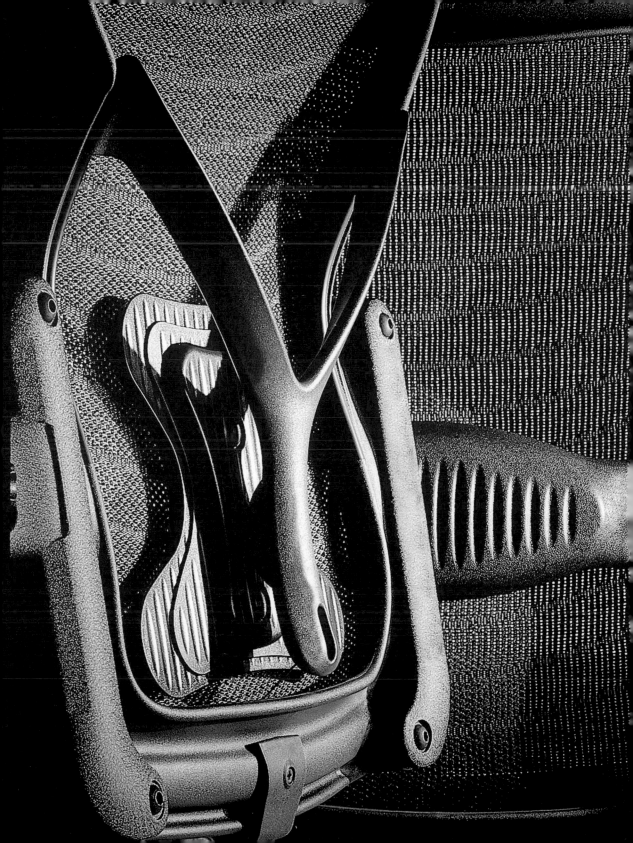

The contender

There are many materials that have applications and formulations that are so diverse it is impossible to categorize them in a straightforward way. Surlyn® is one of these. It is one of the big engineering polymer brands from DuPont. An Ionomer resin, Surlyn® has several high-performance characteristics that make it valuable in a range of applications. It appears in the translucent clarity of the thick, injection molded walls of a perfume bottle, in squeezable, soft, extruded shampoo tubes, and even in the tough, resilient skin on golf balls.

A big marketing drive from plastic producers often results in the benefits of some plastics over other materials being more widely recognized, offering a rationalization of existing materials and components. For example, plastics such as polypropylene are now widely known to be able to integrate live hinges within their moldings while avoiding using secondary materials. On the other hand, take the case of glass, which, although it can be a super-cheap raw material, can't be formed or molded into complex shapes as easily as plastic.

How the many, diverse advantages of Surlyn®, which exist in a range of applications, are communicated to designers is a problem for the brand owners. It might be simplest to label it as a tough, crystal-clear material with a thousand uses waiting to be explored.

Surlyn® Discovery Kit designed to convey the sensorial characteristics of Surlyn®
Designer: DuPont

Dimensions	Each unit is 100mm long
Key Features	**Outstanding impact toughness**
	Abrasion-resistant
	Scuff-resistant
	Chemical-resistant
	Water-clear transparency and clarity
	High melt strength
More	**www.dupont.com**
Typical Applications	**Dog chews, as an alternative to glass in perfume bottles, the skins of golf balls, hockey helmets, footwear, bodyboards, ten-pin bowling pins, tool handles, glass coating, ski boots, laminating film, automotive fascias, and bath and kitchen door handles.**

Inherent toughness

In metallurgists' terms, the words hardness, toughness, and strength have very specific meanings. Toughness is defined as the ability of a material to absorb energy by plastic deformation—an intermediate characteristic between softness and brittleness. The toughness of a product is characterized by impact strength and is only partly dependent on the material: other contributing factors include the way the component is molded, wall thicknesses, and part geometries. There are also factors such as the working temperature of the product and whether it is reinforced, as many materials can be made using various fibers.

However, there are materials that are tough due to their inherent strength. One of the most common and toughest engineering plastics is polycarbonate, which combines this toughness, stiffness, and strength with a superb optical clarity.

In terms of clarity, polycarbonate can be compared with polystyrene, SAN, acrylic, and PET. For its toughness, it can be compared with acetals. One of the uses of polycarbonate resins is in blending with other plastics, such as ABS and PBT. The toughness of this widely used plastic is put to good use in the everyday application of this children's night-light.

Dimensions	125mm x 80mm x 95mm
Key Features	Tough
	Stiff
	Strong
	Water-like transparency
	Flame-resistant
	Excellent dimensional stability, even at high temperatures
	Good heat resistance up to 257°F (125°C)
	Recyclable
	UV-stable
	Nontoxic
More	www.alessi.com
Typical Applications	The CD and DVD industry is completely reliant on polycarbonates. Other applications include visors and safety helmets, eyewear, kitchen containers, computer housings, architectural glazing, cellphone housings, packaging, automotive headlamps, shatter-resistant waterfountain bottles, riot shields, and vandal-proof glazing. Polycarbonates are also used in the electrical and electronics industries.

Beba children's night-light
Designer: Miriam Mirri
Manufacturer: Alessi

180

Engineering your comfort

Hytrel® is one of the main engineering polymers from DuPont. TPEs (thermoplastic elastomers), as with many other plastics, can be formed into many varieties and forms. From its use as a fiber in industrial textiles, to a replacement metal that exploits its natural springiness, Hytrel® crops up in many unexpected places.

What is particularly interesting—even rebellious—about this design for a pillow by designers Maaike Evers and Mike Simonian is that they take the material out of the traditional context of engineering and into the arena of soft furnishings, challenging the possibilities of plastics in a domestic environment.

The pillows mark a new territory for this prolific material, exploiting its combination of the flexibility of rubbers with the strength and processability of plastic. It also integrates mold-in snap fittings and variable wall thickness, and can withstand repetitive bending. The reduction of mass and surface area also provides an efficient form. This not only results in a long-lasting, durable, and easy-to-clean product, but also provides a new visual language for a very traditional product typology.

Thermoplastic Pillow Collection
Designers: Maaike Evers and
Mike Simonian
Manufacturer: Concept only

Dimensions	350mm x 350mm x 80mm
Key Features	**Combines the moldability of plastics with the flexibility of rubber**
	Highly resistant to flex fatigue, chemicals, abrasion, and tearing
	Interior and exterior use
	Can be blow, injection, and rotational molded, or extruded
	Breathable
More	**www.mikeandmaaike.com**
	plastics.dupont.com

Typical Applications

Hytrel® is a highly morphable material, lending itself to a range of forms that exploit its diverse properties. For example, it has been used as an injection molded bedspring, exploiting its strength and flexibility; in the Herman Miller Aeron® office chair (see page 176), which features Hytrel® fibers to replace foam cushioning in the open structured seat and back panels; and in a breathable layer on bedding such as antiallergenic mattresses, quilts, and pillow covers.

Naturally wearing

Key Features	**Superior strength, as with most composites**
	Natural fibers create a unique aesthetic
	Surface is enhanced with age, as with wood or leather
More	**www.studiorob.co.uk**
Typical Applications	**Scratches, knocks, and chips are hidden by the richness of this naturally decorative material. This makes it suitable for anything that has a lot of "people contact," including flooring and furniture, and personal products, such as briefcases.**

Although it is engineers and scientists who develop new formulas for plastics, it is often left to designers to redefine plastics in the cultural context. Designer Rob Thompson has contributed to the evolution of plastics with his "material memories" project. Dealing with the visible signs of age on a product's surface, Rob has looked at how composite materials can be given the capacity to enhance emotional bonding between product and user.

He explains, "To achieve this, I combined plastic with natural fiber-based materials such as straw, wood shavings, feathers, hemp, and recycled newspaper. This resulted in new and exciting composites that utilize the versatile and moldable qualities of synthetic materials with the ageing, aesthetic qualities of natural fibers."

There are many ways in which these products can be adapted in the future. The look of the material will change as different forms of recycled paper are added, such as used billboards. As the paper and typefaces of newspapers change, so will the composite.

The real benefit of these composites and products is that they look to the future, as opposed to being nostalgic. They are sensitive to our desire for material memories in the fast-developing and transient world of the commodities that surround us.

Material Memories Stools
Designer: Rob Thompson
Client: Self-initiated project

Soluble packaging

One of the disadvantages of plastics is that they have an image problem, particularly in terms of environmental friendliness. However, there are many case studies of new materials that are overcoming the major issue of waste disposal. One of the hottest topics in discussions about environmental issues is materials that degrade, whether through solubility, biodegradation, or photodegradation.

Polyvinyl alcohol (PVA) has been around for some time, and today is commonly seen in the form of detergent dispensers for washing machines. But designers have yet to embrace the possibilities of this valuable technology whereby products dissolve in water, having performed their primary function, and leave nothing behind.

Although most of the existing applications are in packaging, there is a constant stream of new developments within water-soluble and other degradable materials. There is no reason why they can't be used for injection moldable or extruded products.

This image of cradlewrap illustrates an application for PVA as a packaging material. It combines a highly impact-resistant structure with a PVA material, which either dissolves in water or is compostable. Taking less than a minute to dissolve in warm tap water, it disintegrates from a thin plastic material to a slippery gel that consists of nothing but carbon dioxide and water.

Key Features	Biodegradable
	Environmentally sound
	Nonhazardous
	Solubility can be controlled by hot or cold water
	Good resistance to chemicals
	Nontoxic residue after it dissolves
	Can offer good degree of transparency
	Good tensile strength and elasticity
	Printable
	Offers user-controllable solubility
More	www.amtrexintl.com
	www.stanelco.devisland.net
	www.stanelcoplc.com
Typical Applications	Applications range from the soap containers for washing machines to edible films. Industrial uses include pharmaceuticals, washaway labels, hospital laundry bags where contaminated clothes can be disposed of without human contact, and public toilet seat protectors. It is also being explored as an alternative to traditional gelatin-based pill capsules, veterinary applications, and plant pesticide capsules that dissolve to release the pesticide into the soil.

CradleWrap water-soluble packing material

Industrial netting is a highly underrated semi-formed material. It has many advantages: it is lightweight, strong, and uses very little material. It is for these reasons that nets are used in everything from packaging oranges to protecting your bottles in duty-free.

In terms of forming, it is extruded into tubes. As with many many types of netting, the rhomboidal structure allows for a natural ability of the net when stretched to conform to the most economical shape, wrapping and hugging itself around items of any shape.

In this packaging design for retailer John Lewis, the netting was used to overcome the problem of how to enclose a set of large, domestic cleaning products in a package that was not excessive in scale, cost, or materials. The products' retail price was a major issue, as these items were designed to appeal to people setting up their first home. The simple color and aesthetics of the products were also selling points, as was the ability to see them in the package. Traditional board materials were rejected due to the cost and quantity of material that would have been needed for each set. However, the combination of the cardboard tray and polypropylene netting provided a strong, cheap, and transparent alternative that allowed for branding, and which also allowed for an integral handle to carry the products with.

Form-hugging

Packaging for Essentials
cleaning products
Designers: Pearce Marchbank
and Chris Lefteri
Client: John Lewis Partnership

Key Features	Contents are exposed but still protected
	Good strength-to-weight ratio
	Can fit any form
	Available in a range of diameters
More	www.tenax.net
Typical Applications	This grade of polypropylene net is used for all types of restraining nets for industrial and horticultural applications, including Christmas tree netting, and nets for pallet loads. Other nets are used for protecting industrial components, for packaging of fruit and vegetables, toys, and even as sponge nets.

Chocolates tray
made from Plantic
water-soluble plastic

Plastic

187

The technology that enables us to manufacture products has developed over thousands of years, allowing evolutions of new methods and techniques and the introduction of completely new ways to make our objects quicker, cheaper, and in larger volumes. It is only recently that we have had to consider the other side of the coin, which is what happens when we throw these objects away. It is the realization that we have become too good at making things faster and cheaper that has prompted research into ways in which materials can have their lives extended or eradicated.

Wash it away

At the very heart of the definition of plastics is the ability of materials to be easily transformed from one state, usually liquid, to another. In virtually all cases, this transition is used to make parts. Plantic® demonstrates the increasing number of applications where the process of transformation is reversed and is used to destroy and safely dispose of the product. Plantic® is as versatile as traditional plastics; it also looks and feels the same. The difference lies in the fact that Plantic® is made from starch, requiring less than a cob of corn to make a chocolate box tray, and, importantly, it dissolves in water.

The makers, Plantic Technologies, relate the biodegradability rate of the plastic with that of household food scraps. Plantic® can be put into the garden composting heap or simply thrown in your trashcan, where you can be assured that it will disappear forever.

Key Features	**Biodegradable**
	Environmentally sound
	Nonhazardous
	Nontoxic residue after it dissolves
More	**www.plantic.com.au**
Typical Applications	**A large market for Plantic® appears to be for trays in the confectionery industry. However, Plantic® can be used to injection mold just about anything, from children's toys to car parts.**

188

Can the can

Dimensions	260mm x 275mm x 405mm
Key Features	**Waxy**
	Easy to mold
	Tough at low temperatures
	Low-cost
	Flexible
	Good chemical-resistance
More	**hugojamson@hotmail.com**
	www.rotomolding.org
Typical Applications	**A number of large-scale children's toys are made from HDPE. Other products include chemical drums, toys, household and kitchenware, cable insulation, carrier bags, automobile fuel tanks, furniture, and the iconic Tupperware.**

Watering can
Designer: Hugo Jamson
Client: Concept project

As environmental issues become increasingly mainstream, so too are the related products that are available to consumers. Products and services are emerging that combine aesthetic pleasure with a measure of ethical fulfilment.

This project looks at how one of the most banal object typologies could merge with an environmental activity to produce a new hybrid. This watering can-cum-trashcan is based on the observation that a watering can often becomes the place in the home where we store and reuse waste water: black tea and coffee; water from boiling or steaming; water from vases of flowers; rainwater, and so on—all of which is good for our plants.

The project addresses the question of what a product might look like if it was to be both liquid trashcan and watering can. The unique aesthetic is driven by its inviting, flared spout, which embraces this new function. As well as acknowledging that there is something good in dirty water, its aesthetic reflects designers' growing acceptance that environmental products need not look like they should sit in a shed at the back of the yard.

Plastic from corn

**Cup and fork made from
Naturework® PLA**

"Your food comes from nature; so does your container," proclaims the NatureWorks® website. More and more major plastics producers are having to address environmental issues with regard to their materials. One of the largest sectors for new development is in the area of degradable plastics and plastics from renewable sources.

NatureWorks® PLA is a technology based on the ability to extract the starch from corn and other plants to make polyactide (PLA) polymer. Once the corn has been milled, the starch that is present is separated from the raw material. Unrefined dextrose is produced from this starch. The dextrose is then turned into lactic acid, using a similar process to that for making wine and beer. This dextrose is the same lactic acid that is found in food additives and also in human muscle tissue. Then, through a special condensation process, a cyclic intermediate dimer, also known as lactide, is formed. The lactide, which is the monomer, is purified through vacuum distillation. The process is completed by polymerization, which happens through a solvent-free melt process.

The ultimate aim of the manufacturer of NatureWorks®, Cargill Dow, is to produce PLA more cheaply than PET resin and become a substitute for polyethylene. Concentrating on the disposable cutlery and packaging markets, the material helps give integrity to an industry that is generally lacking in environmental credibility.

The products have all the elements you would expect of a packaging material, with high clarity and hinges. To all intents and purposes, it would be indistinguishable from a standard product. However, apart from the injection molded products, PLA can be modified to produce a variety of applications such as fibers, foams, emulsions, and chemical intermediaries.

Key Features	Comes from an annually renewable source
	Stiffness and processing temperatures similar to polyolefin resins
	Compostable
	Good clarity
	Good surface finish
	Low odor
More	www.natureworksllc.com
Typical Applications	Blow molded bottles, water-based emulsions, clothing, carpet tiles, rigid thermoformed food and beverage containers, diapers, adhesives, and geo textiles.

Personal mass-production

Provista® is a brand of PETG (polyethylene terephthalate glycol) copolyester from Eastman Chemicals. It was developed for use in extrusions that required optical clarity, toughness, and flexibility. All these properties are evident in Tom Dixon's Fresh Fat range of products.

Beyond the choice of plastic material, what makes this project especially interesting is the combination of a high-volume, mass-production process, and the interpretation of plastic as a handmade craft project. There are many examples of designers using plastic in a craft-like process, but here Tom Dixon uses a high-volume machine as his tool. This unorthodox approach contradicts preconceived notions of plastic as the material of mass-production.

The project provides a new opportunity for combining machine and hand production, in a method that might be closer to making food than plastic, allowing for the personalization of a mass-production process. If there were ever a project that epitomized the visual interpretation of plastic processing, this would rank highly. In its tangled, spaghetti-like form, it expresses the simple reason why plastic is so good at the job of forming shapes. When heated, this pliable, gooey material takes on whatever shape contains it and it stays that way when it cools.

Dimensions	**430mm x 900mm x 560mm**
Key Features	**Gleaming transparency and clarity**
	High-gloss surface
	Does not stress-whiten
	Toughness with flexibility
	Ease of processing and fabrication
	Excellent chemical-resistance
	Environmental advantages: has no plasticizers or halogen-containing compounds, and when burned produces no toxic substances
	FDA compliance for food-contact applications
More	**www.eastman.com**
	www.tomdixon.net
Typical Applications	**Provista® was developed specifically for extruding into profiles where high clarity and finish were important. Its applications include food packaging, furniture, and point of sale.**

Fresh Fat Coffee Table
Designer: Tom Dixon
Manufacturer: Tom Dixon

Rubber-cut fabrics
Designer: Lauren Moriarty
Client: Self-initiated project

3D fabrics

With an emphasis on the constant development of new ways to work with materials, designer Lauren Moriarty has mixed contemporary textiles with product design to create a fresh and original approach. Combining a foam material and laser-cutting, Moriarty has built a range of patterns that explores the use of rubber and plastics to create a modern take on traditional textile techniques.

She says: "Many of the pieces I produce are laser-cut before being molded into shape. The advantage of laser-cutting is the very intricate detail that can be achieved. The cut layers are constructed into 3D pieces and take the form of lighting, cushions, and interior cubes. These 3D 'fabrics' are squashable and have great tactile appeal. The single-layer fabrics relate to the patterns found in lace and constructed textiles, and address the aim of finding new ways to explore textile design using materials not often associated with the subject."

Moriarty's approach to experimentation and the resulting flexible, soft, semi-organic, open-cell foam structures and flat patterns define a new application for foams.

Dimensions	**2mm thick x 500mm width x 1,000mm length**
Key Features	**Lightweight**
	Flexible
	Can be produced in a range of materials
	Cushioning
More	**www.laurenmoriarty.co.uk**
Typical Applications	**Cushions, lighting, and interior paneling.**

Reinventing jewelry

This project is a wonderful combination of material and production, and a great example of a cross-referencing of products. Combining high- and low-value objects, the Postcardring© brings a new meaning to the whole concept of value.

Designer Barbara Schmidt defines her collection of patented, wearable plastic postcards as "spontaneous happiness, colorful sensibility, and playful lightness combined with the joy of giving and decorating oneself. This is the spectrum of positive emotions appealed to by the newly developed ring postcard."

The rings can be sent in an envelope and brought to life by popping out the ring from its die-cut postcard and hooking the ends together to wrap it around the finger. The project encompasses a range of sheet materials and colors from which the rings can be ordered. Apart from them being a completely new expression of jewelry, the products make a clever connection between low-tech die-cutting technology and do-it-yourself assembly.

Postcardring©
Designer: Barbara Schmidt
Manufacturer: Barbara Schmidt

Dimensions	230mm x 120mm
Key Features	Can be heat-welded, ultrasonically welded, riveted, stitched, and embossed
	Easy and versatile processing
	Excellent resistance to chemicals
	Excellent live hinge potential
	Low water absorption and permeability to water vapor
	Recyclable
	Very cheap tooling
	Manual assembly process
	High print adhesion
	Virtually impossible to tear
	Low-density
More	www.barbara-schmidt-schmuck.de
Typical Applications	Die-cut polypropylene is huge business; it is used in everything from high- and low-end packaging, stationery, table mats, and folio cases, to the more design-led applications of furniture and lighting.

Dimensions	730mm x 440mm x 440mm
Key Features	Virtually limitless possibilities of shapes
	Available in a range of materials
	Low capital investment
More	www.patrickjouin.com
	www.materialise.com
Typical Applications	Car manufacturers, engineers, designers, and architects use stereo lithography to produce prototypes and concept models. In manufacturing it is used to create patterns and masters for melds and short run final products. Recently, surgeons have also begun to use this technology to recreate affected anatomy in preparation for complicated operations.

Objects to go

Solid chair
Designer: Patrick Jouin
Manufacturer: 3D Systems

Rapid prototyping is changing the world of production, as it allows for previously impossible forms to be produced as multiples. The tool provides freedom from the constraints of the manufacturing process to offer a new world of possible objects.

In the last 10 years, there have been a number of projects exploring the various forms that this exciting technology takes. There is an ever-increasing number of methods within this manufacturing family. Most common types use lasers and photosensitive resin for stereolithography—laminated paper built up in layers and ink-jet. This project uses a range of powder and liquid polymers to create the various pieces from inputted designs.

In a process that is so forward-looking, there is nevertheless a reference to the past in the sense that objects are created from solid materials in a one-off. As someone who is excited by the production of objects, I think this has to be one of the most intriguing areas to watch, where complex structures are slowly brought to life from a solid mass over a period of hours. Objects reveal themselves like magic.

Rapid prototyping may have the same sort of impact that 3D modeling on the computer had in terms of changing the form of products. It will be interesting to see how the speed at which 3D experiments can be made will change the look of products.

If you find a forgotten product typology that is mundane and everyday in its use and redesign it to give it a distinctive visual personality, you are halfway to creating a unique and recognizable product. If design has now fully explored every part of the product world for human beings, then it is now engaging with the animal kingdom and applying contemporary aesthetics to cats, dogs, and chickens.

The Eglu chicken coop, made by Omlet, is made from rotational molded polyethylene. This material is similar to PVC in the volume of its consumption worldwide and its availability in an extensive range of varieties. Some formulas of polyethylene are bendable and supple, while others are rigid; some are highly resistant to breaking, whereas others are easily broken. However, as a family, polyethylenes are characterized by chemical resistance and toughness. High-density polyethylene (HDPE) is used in the Eglu because of its stiffness and strength.

Apart from being one of a kind and providing a giant leap in chicken architecture, the Eglu is a wonderful advert for rotational molding in polyethylene. The bright, contemporary colors and large moldings are the perfect opportunity to show one of the key advantages of this prolific partnership of material and molding technique.

Eglu chicken coop
Designers: James Tuthill, Johannes Paul,
Simon Nichols, and William Windham
Manufacturer: Omlet

Dimensions	700mm x 800mm x 800mm
Key Features	**Waxy**
	Easy to mold
	Tough at low temperatures
	Low-cost
	Flexible
	Good chemical-resistance
More	**www.omlet.co.uk**
Typical Applications	**A number of large-scale children's toys are made from HDPE. Other products include chemical drums, toys, household and kitchenware, cable insulation, carrier bags, car fuel tanks, furniture, and Tupperware.**

Chicken architecture

There is one good reason why Lego® is made from ABS (acrylonitrile butadiene styrene). Apart from the fact that it has a high-gloss surface, and is cost-effective and easy to mold, it is also one of the toughest commodity plastics on the market.

Lego® is one of the world's favorite toys. The name dates back to 1934. It is a combination of the Danish words "leg" and "godt," which translates into English as "play-well" and into Latin as "I put together." It is a product that has embraced plastic and has used advances in the material to evolve the brand into a series of products that keep up to date with children's imaginations and trends in toys.

On average, for every person on Earth there are 52 Lego® bricks. This proliferation has made it an icon of plastic. The bricks require an extremely high degree of manufacturing tolerances—0.002mm—for the "stud-and-tube" principle to work. That process keeps the 400,000,000 children and adults who play with Lego® bricks every year happy, and makes sure that they always, always stick together.

Lego® bricks
Designer: Lego
Manufacturer: Lego

Tough

Key Features	High-impact strength, even at low temperatures
	Low-cost
	Versatile production
	Good resistance to chemicals
	Good dimensional stability
	Scratch-resistant
	Flame-resistant
	Can achieve a high gloss
	Excellent mechanical strength and stiffness
More	www.lego.com
	www.geplastics.com
	www.basf.com
Typical Applications	A huge range, from cellphone casings, where it is combined with PC to make even tougher moldings, to shower trays and food processors. ABS is also used in a whole range of white goods and automotive consoles.

Environmental PVC

Polyvinyl chloride (PVC) was one of the first widely available plastics, and it still occupies one of the largest areas of plastics consumed worldwide. It is probably the plastic that, along with polythene, has most filtered into common language. However, since the 1980s, PVC has developed a reputation as being an environmentally unfriendly material. These concerns come from several fronts. The first is the use of a chlorine compound that forms such a large part of PVC's composition. Unlike many other plastics, PVC is based on the use of approximately 50 percent petrochemicals; the other half is made of a chlorine-based compound. This marks one of its key advantages to producers, as the price of PVC is not as heavily based on price fluctuations of oil. However, the downside is that the production of PVC produces harmful dioxins.

The second main environmental issue is based on the use of the stabilizers and plasticizers in the production of the material. Stabilizers are used to impede degradation and plasticizers to increase flexibility. Both of these additives have problems. Stabilizers use heavy metals such as lead and barium, and plasticizers containing hormone disrupters.

There are moves to reduce these various problems by the manufacturers: they can reduce the amount of dioxins being produced and can use organic stabilizers. The PVC industry's defense lies in what they claim is the low level of risk and likely exposure to these substances, and the fact that PVC has been used in the medical industry for many years for blood bags, where the use of plasticizers has been shown to extend the shelf life of blood.

Designed by Karim Rashid and using an environmentally friendly form of PVC, this dog toy is the lifestyle alternative to a wooden stick. It expresses the idea that a product for a pet can also be something that the owner would enjoy possessing. This product has a fantastic shape that you would not mind having lying around at home.

Dimensions	**200mm x 200mm x 35mm**
Key Features	**Easy to form**
	Cheap
	Easy to color
	Water- and chemical-resistant
	Available in a variety of forms
More	**www.ecvm.org**
	www.karimrashid.com
	www.forthedogs.com
Typical Applications	**It is difficult to summarize the versatility of this material and the markets it is used in. Applications include dip-molded bicycle handles, drain pipes, flooring, cabling, artificial skin in emergency burns treatment, sun visors, domestic appliances, raincoats, credit cards, and inflatable toys. Unplasticized or rigid PVC (PVC-U) is used extensively in building applications such as window frames.**

Dog bone
Designer: Karim Rashid
Manufacturer: For the Dogs

Is it a tape, is it a fabric, or is it a plastic molding? Whatever category it fits into, Hook and Loop (more commonly know as Velcro®) is a product that offers a great case study for a use of plastic. It is also one of the most useful inventions of the twentieth century.

It is well known that the structure of Velcro® fibers is based on a mechanical fixing that is borrowed from nature, where the tiny hooks—commonly known as burrs—found on the end of some seed pods attach the seed more easily to an implantable surface that might brush past. It was this observation that led to Velcro®'s name being patented in the early 1950s by Swiss engineer George de Mestral: the name derives from the French words for velvet (velour), and hook (crochet).

This product has been used in both everyday contexts and advanced applications, allowing us to create new functions and products. It is another product that demonstrates the flexibility of plastics, and is unique in that it crosses the boundary between fabric, tape, and molded plastic. It also provides a case study because it appeals on so many levels: it combines the beauty of a simple observation into a product that has filtered into every possible area of application.

There are variations on standard Velcro® available, including conductive Velcro® and a super-strong product branded under the name Dual Lock™. Instead of the hook-and-loop principle, this relies on a series of tiny mushrooms to join the two identical halves of the material together. In all versions of the material, this is a product that has brought new potential to the use of pliable plastics to be used as fixings.

Peelable fastener

Key Features	Strong
	Lightweight
	Durable
	Washable
	Available in a range of grades
More	www.velcro.com
	www.3m.com
Typical Applications	Plastics have allowed for a mass of new types of fixing mechanisms that exploit the flexibility and resilience of plastics. Velcro® has an incalculable number of applications in which it is used, ranging from wearable to industrial. 3M, the makers of Dual Lock™, claim that its product has five times the tensile strength of standard Velcro®. It is used to invisibly attach doors and panels, headliners to cars, and in other applications that require superior strength.

3M Dual Lock
Manufacturer: 3M

Presto Digital Bracelet
Designer: Scott Wilson
Manufacturer: Nike

Most products use plastic because it serves the purpose of the lowest common denominator. These are products that have no real relationship between material and aesthetics: they are merely the most convenient material in which to execute the form. But then there are products that celebrate the use of plastic, where the shape, color, material, and function combine to reveal an object that seems to have been born out of the material itself—a product that could not have been made with any other material. These Presto watches by Nike are beautiful products in which the use of plastic oozes the sensual quality of a high-gloss, polished, transparent surface.

Scott Wilson, the designer of the watch, is building up a collection of products that show a complete understanding of how plastic can be utilized in an intelligent and beautiful way within a range of everyday products. Surprisingly, the candy-color aesthetic is not cellulose as might be expected, but a custom-blended nylon 12, a material used in many sports eyewear frames.

The form defines the relationship between product and wearer, with the simple clasp contributing to the visual language of the form and exploiting the toughness of nylon. To produce the watches, each band is molded, tumbled, and hand-polished to achieve the smooth finish and fluid "techno-organic" aesthetic.

Dimensions	**13mm x 28.5mm diameter**
Key Features	**Extremely high bending strength**
	Excellent toughness
	Exceptional resistance to chemicals
	Lightweight
	High transparency
	Approved for water temperature up to 185°F (85°C)
More	**www.emsgrivory.com**
	www.studiomod.com
Typical Applications	**Applications exist in areas that exploit this grade of nylon's extremely high impact strength and high optical clarity. Products include frames for safety glasses, lenses in optical glasses, instrument panels on cars, wing mirror housings, and cellphone housings.**

High bending strength

Molded origami

the surprising
FOLD HANGER

Polypropylene (PP) has been a relatively new introduction to plastics. Originally developed in the 1950s, this commodity plastic occupies one of the largest segments in the plastic industry.

Polypropylene is as common in its molded form as it is in its die-cut sheet form, where it offers the designer a halfway point between folded paper and a fully tooled-up, molded product. Like a piece of clever origami, this fold-up coat hanger bridges these areas. As a raw material, polypropylene is relatively cheap and easy to process. It is also one of the best materials for creating live hinges, which is the prominent feature in this little gadget.

The product is one of those small discoveries that you come across that offer little in the way of real value, but provide a small narrative on top of a great case study of the performance of certain plastics. It captures within its creases and hinges a quality that I think is unique to plastic. It is a tactile, playful, and almost disposable example of the banal nature of how plastic can do so many things that we often don't know what to do with. It is part of the world of plastic gadgets, with a combination of origami and surprise that transforms the product from a small rectangle 120mm x 80mm into a rigid coat hanger for the executive nomad.

Dimensions	**Expands from 120mm x 80mm**
Key Features	**Can be flexed thousands of times without breaking**
	High heat-resistance
	Excellent resistance to chemicals
	Low water absorption and permeability to water vapor
	Good balance between toughness, stiffness, and hardness
	Easy and versatile processing
	Relatively low-cost
	Low-density
	Low coefficient of friction
More	**www.basf.com**
Typical Applications	**Garden furniture, food packaging, general household goods, dispensing lids for bathroom shower products, toothpaste tube lids, most products with an in-built hinge, bottle crates, and tool handles.**

Thin and limp

PVC (polyvinyl chloride) is a commodity plastic that occupies one of the largest areas of plastics consumed worldwide. It is a material with many personalities, as it can be treated as thermoplastic, elastomer, and thermoset plastics. In its highly stiff and rigid form, it is known as the poor man's engineering plastic, but it can also be as flexible and limp as a piece of leather. Perhaps it was this analogy that prompted the use of PVC in this shoe by designer Yves Béhar.

The Learning Shoe, which was commissioned by the San Francisco Museum of Modern Art, explores the relationship between a wearable garment and a computer chip. Data is collected about the wearer's feet and walking style, and a smart sole adapts the shoe based on this information. Like a high-tech slipper from the next century, the form is like a seamless extension of the foot that wraps itself around the body like a piece of leather, while at the same time conforming to the soft, glossy language of plastic.

Dimensions	**285.75mm x 114.3mm x 63.5mm**
Key Features	**Easy to form**
	Cheap
	Easy to color
	Water- and chemical-resistant
	Available in a variety of forms
More	**www.fuseproject.com**
Typical Applications	**It is difficult to summarize briefly the versatility of this material and the markets it is used in. Some applications include dip-molded bicycle handles, drain pipes, flooring, cabling, artificial skin in emergency burns treatment, sun visors, domestic appliances, raincoats, credit cards, and inflatable toys. Unplasticized or rigid PVC (PVC-U) is used extensively in building applications such as window frames.**

Learning Shoe
Designer: Yves Béhar
Client: San Francisco Museum
of Modern Art

207 Wood

Byron armchair
Designer: Philipp Mainzer
Client: E15

Modern luxury

Walnut is as famous for its natural decorative qualities as it is for its fruit. From Queen Anne furniture to the interiors of modern luxury cars, walnut is one of the most desirable veneers.

This uncompromising range of furniture uses neutral steel and aluminum to contrast and enhance the rich grain and natural color variation in this type of walnut. In contrast to the highly decorative nature of the wood, the simple, nondecorative structures allow the natural beauty of the coarse texture, cracks, and knots of the walnut to be displayed.

The walnut tree also produces tannin as an astringent and as an antidote to some poisons. Procured by distilling the leaves, tannin is often used to soften leather. Walnut kernels are also processed to make oil.

Dimensions	Byron armchair: 840mm x 680mm x 620mm
	Fara sideboard: 1,800mm x 450mm x 675mm
Key Features	Color can vary
	Straight or wavy grain with a coarse texture
	Excellent steam bending properties
	Easy to work and polishes to a high finish
More	www.e15.com
Typical Applications	Decorative veneers, gun and rifle stocks, shop fittings, furniture, interior joinery, and car interiors.

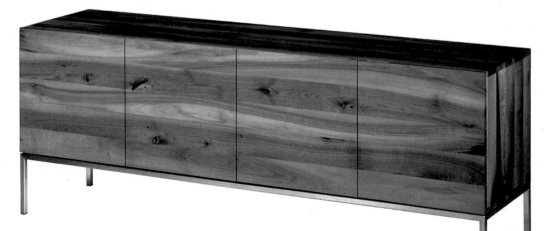

Fara sideboard
Designer: Philipp Mainzer
Client: E15

Fine-tuning

Beech is one of the most widely-used woods. It is strong, elastic, finishes well, and is easily worked. Inspiration for the Momentos beech bureau came from the rather strange-looking furniture featured in *Saint Jerome in his Study*, a Renaissance painting by Antonello da Messina. All features deemed superfluous to the function of the bureau have been stripped away. The end of the shutter is linked to a small pull-out extension table giving the bureau a valuable surprise element. When work has finished for the day, everything can be put away, "out of sight, out of mind."

This type of beech has a strength comparable to European ash. Its uniform grain and pattern do not contrast with the color of the wood itself. It also has a uniform density making it relatively easy to work, i.e. cut, machine, sand, or sculpt. These qualities are demonstrated in the design of the Momentos which boasts a finely machined 20mm-deep routed groove that sits a mere 8mm from the circular edge.

Momentos bureau
Designer: KC Lo

Dimensions	1,000mm x 400mm x 1,000mm
Key Features	Close, consistent straight grain
	Excellent strength
	Good workability
	Can produce an excellent finish
	Excellent steam bending properties
More	www.mosstimber.co.uk
	kc@netmatters.co.uk
Typical Applications	Beech has many applications including shoe lasts and shoe trees, tool handles, toys, furniture, brush handles, cabinets, sports goods, turned products, kitchen utensils, and parts for musical instruments.

Chair with Holes
Designer: Gijs Bakker

The whole story

Maple is an extremely hard, creamy-white wood;
an obvious choice for a functional object with
so many holes, but these holes are more than
decorative. They hide the logic of the structure,
a matrix of informed decisions.

"I wanted to make it lighter, both visually and
physically, so I drilled some holes in it," says Gijs
Bakker. The size of each hole corresponds to the
parts of the chair which require the greatest and the
least amount of support. The larger the hole, the less
stress is placed on that particular area. Post-drilling,
the chair lost almost a third of its original weight.

Dimensions	**440mm x 430mm x 780mm**
Key Features	**High resistance to abrasion and wear**
	Difficult to work
	Good for steam bending
	Reasonable staining and finishing
	Fine and even texture
	Medium density
	Usually straight-grained
	Needs to be pre-bored for nailing and screwing
More	**www.droogdesign.nl**
Typical Applications	**Used in flooring for squash courts, bowling alleys, and roller-skating rinks. Also used in shoe lasts, rollers for textile production, furniture, turned ware, and a maple syrup derivative.**

Natural weatherability

Teak is often associated with premium garden furniture and decking on yachts. Its distinguishing features of weatherability and hardness make it a natural choice for use in the great outdoors. The secret of its good weathering properties lies in the natural oils that clog the pores, eliminating the need for preservatives and making it maintenance-free. It is similar to iroko in this way, which is often used as an alternative.

Unfortunately, buying teak is not so easy on the conscience. Today, most teak comes from colonial plantations in Java, where elephants are still used to move the logs and where a large proportion of the timber is not certified.

Dimensions	900mm x 600mm x 750mm
Key Features	**Medium density**
	Good for steam bending
	Excellent dimensional stability in a wide range of temperatures
	Good resistance to chemicals
	Moderately easy to work
More	**www.tribu.be**
	www.sydenhams.co.uk
	www.moderngarden.co.uk
Typical Applications	**Teak is a useful material for ship building and cabinet making. It is also used for garden furniture, chemical containers, lab benches, and decking**

Trolley table
Designer: Wim Seyers
Client: Tribu

Strong and flexible

From transport to weapons of war, ash is well known for its flexibility and is, in fact, one of the toughest English timbers around. It is also an excellent shock absorber.

These stools by Hans Sandgren Jakobsen were designed for the Walk the Plank project where 40 designers were each given a plank of wood from which to produce a seating item. "It was a luxury to be able to develop a product without any consideration for commercial interest. It was a playful assignment and a great opportunity to go all the way, to go crazy," explains Jakobsen.

The Rockable and the Unrockable stools explore new ways for people to sit in a unique and sculptural structure. The Rockable stool is made from 37 staves fixed into a circular foot, at the end of which is a turned knob. The Unrockable follows the same principle, but instead has 35 staves in a rectangular base.

The Rockable (top) and the
Unrockable (bottom)
Designer: Hans Sandgren Jakobsen
Manufacturer: HB Trædrejeri and
Lars Verner

Key Features	Straight-grained with a coarse texture
	Excellent workability when steamed
	Outstanding toughness
	Good flexibility
More	www.davidcolwell.com
	www.hans-sandgren-jakobsen.com
Typical Applications	Railway coach vehicle construction; hockey sticks; gym equipment; tool handles such as hammers, shovels, and axes; oars; early cars; and aircraft.

Fine cabinet wood

**Eighteen cabinet
Designer:
John Makepeace**

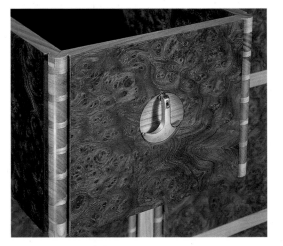

"Something that interests me is using materials for their best properties." says John Makepeace. Makepeace is one of the foremost designers and makers of wooden furniture in the world. He set up the Parnham Trust in 1977, where he teaches wooden-furniture design and continues to inspire and enthuse with his own design ranges. His innovative use of timber in the construction of Hooke Park College demonstrates his interest and responsibility toward the use of sustainable materials in architecture.

His pieces are a celebration of wood in all its functional and aesthetic forms. Each item of furniture may involve the use of several types of timber. The main frame and drawers of the Eighteen cabinet are made of English cherry, for its structural qualities and interesting color. The surface is elm and the drawers slide in and out on runners made of hornbeam, chosen for its ability to take up the friction.

Dimensions	**780mm x 420mm x 1,400cm**
Key Features	**Good bending and working properties**
	Similar strength to oak
	Excellent for turning
	Straight-, fine-, and even-textured grain
More	**www.johnmakepeace.com**
Typical Applications	**Cherry is commonly used in furniture, tableware, and musical instrument parts.**

Varied cherry

The Whole Chair by David Landess is made from hundreds of different-sized blocks of cherry wood. It was constructed on its side from a loop form and then turned upright when the final form was completed. "The Whole Chair was influenced by the idea of using the ubiquitous brick; a very simple and ancient way of producing a structure and perhaps the earliest example we have of mass-production as a tool and process," says Landess.

Whole Chair
Designer: David Landess

Key Features	Good bending and working properties
	Similar strength to oak
	Excellent for turning
	Straight-, fine-, and even-textured grain
Typical Applications	Cherry is commonly used in furniture, tableware, and musical instrument parts

Take one tree

One Tree is an ongoing project, initiated by Gary Olson and Peter Toaig in Tasmania, where different uses of oak are explored and developed. The One Tree story began in November 1998 when a group of craftspeople, artists, designers, and community members came together to develop and demonstrate a more sustainable and positive future for Tasmania's forests. Their attention focused on one particular 170-year-old oak tree that would otherwise have been made into woodchip. The money they raise is used to extend the One Tree example to revaluing whole forests.

By involving people from a range of creative disciplines, the project raises awareness of the rich diversity of uses that oak offers. From the bark, which has been used to make a dress and tan leather, and its leaves which are used to make paper, to its sawdust, used to smoke ham, and a wood-ash glaze for ceramic pots, nothing in this tree has been overlooked as a potential resource.

Dimensions	**1,080mm x 180mm x 60mm each**
Key Features	**Coarse texture**
	Straight and rich grain
	Good workability and finishing
	Good resistance to water
	Excellent for steam bending
More	**www.onetree.org.uk**
Typical Applications	**Oak has a wide variety of uses including furniture, flooring, boat building, wine and whiskey barrels, frames, doors, panelling, pews, and carving.**

One Tree wall boxes
Designer: Gill Wilson

Local resources

Drawing on local resources, design group Droog has applied its highly original interpretation of materials and processes to a unique cultural project.

Droog was commissioned to design a family of products based on the themes of restoration, revival, and innovation that would reflect and revitalize the culture of the area of Oranienbaum in Germany. The abundance of poplar made it the most suitable material for this disposable, wooden orange peeler.

Dimensions	**20mm x 50mm x 120mm**
Key Features	**Pale coloring**
	Tough for its weight
	Good resistance to splintering compared with other softwoods
	Straight- but woolly-grained
	Good workability
	Poor for steam bending
More	**www.droogdesign.nl**
Typical Applications	**Matches, interior joinery, toys, break-blocks for railway wagons, and boxes.**

Portable orange peeler
Designer: Marti Gruixé
Client: Kulturstiftung DessauWorlitz

ORANIENBAUM
PORTABLE ORANGENSCHÄLER

Wooden textiles

The willow tree yields sleek off-shoots and branches that grow in long uninterrupted lengths, making it an ideal material to weave. The many varieties of user-friendly, long, soft fibers don't splinter easily and so can be used for a range of applications. The true definition of wicker is woven willow, and there are two main types of construction used in the ancient process of basket-making. The first uses a frame as a guide for the basket to be built around. The second is the steak and strand method where the basket is created from a base.

Lee Dalby grows and harvests his own ingredients for a range of projects, from baskets to architecture. This is a uniquely honest process where the designer is not only working with the processing materials and converting them into objects, but is also directly involved in growing and harvesting, which he believes is of equal importance for the final products.

"It's important to be involved in the seasonal process. In winter the sap is in the ground and not in the fibers which makes the wood too soft. The branches are bundled to let them dry out ready for working. When they are ready to be woven they are soaked to make them malleable and soft," says Dalby.

Split willow-frame basket

Dimensions	1,350mm x 890mm x 250mm
Key Features	**Straight-, fine- and even-grained**
	Lightweight, resilient, and flexible
	Easily worked
	Poor for steam bending
More	**marshchav@hotmail.com**
Typical Applications	**Cricket bat blades, wickerwork, punnets, clogs, crates, toys, flooring, and moire veneers.**

4lbs per cubic foot

It is easy to forget that the various species of wood around the world and their physical properties are dictated by diverse climatic conditions. Species like bamboo and balsa thrive in warm climates with plenty of rainfall and good drainage, which enable the trees to grow very quickly. This rapid growth produces lightweight wood of such low density that you can push your thumb into it.

Pollinated by tiny seed pods carried and distributed by the wind across the jungle, balsa trees used to be thought of as weeds and still are by some farmers. Within six months of germination the balsa tree can be 10–12 feet tall, and after six years the tree can reach 60 feet and is ready to be cut. If it's harvested too late, the outer wood hardens, leaving the inside of the tree to rot.

Today, most commercial-grade balsa comes from Ecuador. Here, balsa is known as boya, meaning buoy. The word balsa derives from the Spanish word for raft, reflecting its excellent floating properties.

Balsawood surfboard

Key Features	**Highest strength-to-weight ratio of any wood**
	Absorbs shock and vibration
	Easy to glue and cut
	Excellent buoyancy
	Poor for steam bending
	Extremely easy to work
More	**www.surfspot.co.uk**
Typical Applications	**Model aircraft, speedboats, heat, sound and vibration insulation, buoyancy in lifebelts and water-sports equipment, and theater props.**

Model classics

This straight-grained, fine and even-textured wood is well-known to every design student as one of the most common materials used for model making. Less well-known is Giovanni Sacchi, yet he is generally regarded as one of the masters of wood-modeling.

Over the last 50 years he has worked with some of the most celebrated names in Italian design using predominantly jelutong Fand cembra pine for his miniature models. From his small workshop in Milan, Giovanni has crafted over 25,000 wooden models, including cutlery, computers, electric fans, sewing machines, furniture ranges, architectural models, and lighting designs.

Anyone familiar with jelutong will know the only problem with working it is in tackling the gooey latex knots in the middle of a plank, which hinders the progress of any slick model. But latex does serve its own purpose of course—feeding the huge market for chewing gum.

Key Features	**Plain, straight, fine, and even grain**
	Medium density
	Low stiffness
	Very easy to work
	Good finishing properties
More	**www.mosstimber.co.uk**
Typical Applications	**Jelutong is used for pattern making, model making, drawing boards, wood carving, wooden clogs, interior joinery, and latex for chewing gum.**

Prototype models made in Jelutong
Designer: Giovanni Sacchi

Luxury

Hickory is an exotic wood with a very high density and an ability to remain sturdy when formed from a thin cross-section. Traditionally used by decadent Victorian gentlemen to show off their status, walking sticks range from plain and simple to incredibly ornate.

These lavish and ostentatious displays of material luxury were the must-haves of their day, well before the branding revolution of the late twentieth century. They are admired for the beauty of their surface, coloring, and grain, as well as for their perfect harmony of weight, proportion, and finish. Satin-smooth and expertly-machined, these simple pieces just yearn to be touched.

Hickory crook

Dimensions	**Height: 920mm**
Key Features	**High density**
	Straight grain with coarse texture
	High bending strength
	High shock resistance
	Excellent steam bending properties
	Difficult to work
	Nondurable
More	**www.james-smith.co.uk**
Typical Applications	**Hickory is used for tool handles, hammers, axes, baseball bats, lacrosse sticks, ladder rungs, and drum sticks.**

Natural lubrication

Lignum vitae is a super wood; it boasts characteristics closer to other materials than to its own material family. This tough, self-lubricating, exceptionally dense wood is unique; it is the only wood that sinks in water.

One of its early uses was in mechanical applications. It was used in bearings for propeller shafts in ships which took advantage of its natural lubrication. This quality was also exploited in clocks in the eighteenth century; lignum vitae was used to replace metal parts that needed lubricating with animal fat, creating clocks of incredible precision.

When first cut, this wood is soft and reasonably easy to work, but on contact with air it becomes increasingly hard. More contemporary uses are for croquet mallets, and until recently, it was often used for hammer heads.

Key Features	Self-lubricating
	Good for turning
	Excellent durability
	Very difficult to work
	Poor for steam bending
	High resistance to chemicals
Typical Applications	Traditionally used for mallet heads, wooden bowls, wheel guides, pestles and mortars, early clock mechanisms, hammer heads, and pulley sheaths for ships.

Soft hardwood

Known as the "carver's wood" or basswood, lime is a timber that for thousands of years has provided craftsmen with the perfect physical characteristics for carving. Like balsa wood, lime is one of those timbers which provides the contradicting notion of being a soft hardwood.

With its pale, creamy-yellow-colored close grain and resistance to splitting, lime is used as the main timber in the playful Vine chair by John Makepeace. The chair offers a contemporary and relevant example of this wood, which demonstrates its key features. Its good dimensional stability, its ability to be easily worked by hand, and its pale coloring, which can easily be stained, are all features that are utilized in the chair. The seat and back provide structural elements, and are made from several planks of wood glued together and carved. The decorative qualities of the chair extend the function, by referring to nature and the associations of relaxing in the garden.

Vine chair
Designer: John Makepeace

Dimensions	550mm x 550mm x 900mm
Key Features	Excellent resistance to splitting
	Easy to work
	Low stiffness
	Can produce a good finish
	Straight-, uniform- and fine-textured grain
More	www.johnmakepeace.com
Typical Applications	Carving, cutting boards for leatherwork and pattern-making, turned products, hat blocks, and artificial limbs.

Key Features	Easy to work
	Straight grain
	Coarse texture
	Strong color variation
	Poor for steam bending
	Highly distinctive aroma
	Fades to silver-gray after weathering
More	www.dunkelman.com
	www.mosstimber.co.uk
Typical Applications	Pencils, beehives, and wardrobes. Inferior grades are used in construction.

The function of smell

Red cedar smells good; the kind of smell that evokes memories. Wood has some of the most natural, beautiful, and tactile surfaces, but for many species, it's the natural aroma that stays with us. The intense relationship between smell and memory that wood generates elevates it to a higher materials league altogether.

So where better to use a wood with a pleasant and distinctive aroma than in a shoetree? Dunkelman & Sons uses a range of woods for its shoetrees. Starting at the lower end, it uses poplar for its exceptional lightness and lime for its clean look, stability, and light weight. At the top end is the aromatic and deodorizing American red cedar.

Apart from the use of this strong, aromatic wood, the other interesting aspect of these shoetrees is in their production. Starting from the toe and working up, card models are used to slowly build up the form, cutting and layering until a model with approximately 15 to 20 sections is produced to make a perfect fit for a shoe. This solid model can then be used on an assymetrical copy lathe to produce each individual tree. Only one model is needed, as the machine can be adjusted to form each shoe size. These wonderful moisture- and smell-absorbing accessories are hand-finished and sanded.

Dense

Compressed laminated
hammer with ash handle
for working hot sheet metal
Manufacturer: Thor Hammer

The hammer has to be one of the few products where development has been almost totally down to the use of new materials. Its form has remained virtually unchanged since it was realized that a hard object tied to a handle could break things more easily than holding a hard rock in the palm of your hand. Today, the only difference is that the rock is made from an assortment of different materials and instead of being tied, is securely attached to the handle.

There are many different kinds of hammers made from specific materials to suit particular purposes. Traditionally, mallets for beating heated steel panels were made of lignum vitae. This is now uneconomical and has been replaced by compressed laminated wood, which has a much higher density.

Key Features	Compression-proof and resistant to wear
	Dimensionally stable
	Noise absorbing
	Insulating
	Resistant to water, oil, diluted acids, and alkaline
More	www.permalidehoplast.co.uk
	www.dehonit.com
	www.thorhammer.com
Typical Applications	Applications where there are no metal parts.

Veneering is centuries old. There are countless examples of decorative coverings that maximize the use of rare woods, either over common timber or board products. During the early days of aircraft manufacture thin ply materials were used to reduce weight.

The Laleggera chair (the range also includes benches, stools, and a table) is an innovative, contemporary example of sheets of wood being used to enhance construction qualities, and combines two totally different materials in a deceptively simple design. These structures use very thin timber and appear to be of a totally wooden construction. However, a closer look reveals that they are made from single sheets of veneer with a plugged hole on the underside to allow for a polyurethane foam injection. The thin veneered sheets are assembled over a solid timber frame before the foam is injected to make the structure rigid. This highly original wood and foam combo has created a light, strong, ergonomic stacking chair.

Wooden skin

Dimensions	530mm x 360mm x 790mm
	Seat height: 460mm
	Weight: 2,390kg
Key Features	Economical use of material
	Excellent strength-to-weight ratio
More	www.aliasdesign.it
Typical Applications	Aircraft construction, decorative inlays, marquetry, plywood, block board, furniture, and doors.

Laleggera chair
Designer: Ricardo Blumer
Client: Alias

Not a wood but certainly a derivative, the fruit of the coconut palm is one of the world's most abundant and unique fruits. Like apple and pear, this fruit-bearing tree is treasured as much, if not more, for its fruit than the wood itself.

The best ideas sometimes arise from restrictive situations. Others work because they take abundant materials and find new applications and contexts for them. The rough hairs that encase the coconut are made into coir—one of the only natural fibers that is rot-resistant—the perfect material for doormats. The fibers can also be formed into insulation boards for use in flooring or ceiling applications, an easy and additive-free production method.

Dimensions	**Individual boards: 1,250mm x 625mm**
	Thicknesses: 13mm, 18mm, 23mm, and 28mm without compression
Key Features	**Excellent durability**
	Rot-resistant
	Good thermal and acoustic insulation
	Environmentally friendly
	Almost odorless
More	**www.coirtrade.com**
	www.coconut.com
	constructionresources.com
	www.fertilefibre.co.uk
Typical Applications	**Rope, yarns, doormats, rugs, water filters, ground erosion control, soundproofing, brush bristles, and plant mulch.**

Sample of coconut fiber board
Supplied by: Construction Resources

Thermal and acoustic insulation

Cooked wood

If you want to avoid the nasty fumes from artificially produced briquettes use natural charcoal. Much of the charcoal currently used for barbecues comes from sources that are difficult to identify and could easily come from endangered trees. The Traditional Charcoal Company uses coppiced wood from well-managed forests. Cooking the charcoal takes two days and begins with stacking logs in a steel kiln, which looks like a giant cooking pot. As the logs burn, the contents sink and are covered and sealed with sand or earth. After cooking for 16 to 18 hours, the charcoal is allowed to cool before being shovelled out, sorted, and packed.

More

**The Traditional Charcoal Company
Cheshire, UK
Tel: +44 (0) 1606 835243**

Charcoal

Chew on this

There are many uses for trees and their fruits that have nothing at all to do with making products or furniture. And not all the edible parts of a tree come from the fruit. This is a surprising use of a resin that comes from inside the wood itself.

Cultural history is filled with references to remedies, ointments, and potions derived from wood—from the use of the ashes of the beech tree for making soap and refining of syrup from the maple tree, to Tencel®, Rayon®, and cellulose for making plastics.

The fine and even texture of jelutong wood is excellent for model making and one of the main uses for its latex is in the production of chewing gum.

Chewing gum

Plastic wood

The future of materials will continue to be heavily influenced by these types of composite, where materials combine to form new ones with multiple personalities. Timbercel® is one of these new materials which will continue to evolve, blurring the boundaries of where one material stops and another begins. It has the efficient mass processability of plastic with the workability of wood: a combination of a polymer resin and between 30 and 50 percent recycled wood flour.

The resulting mix can be best described as plastic wood, which can be extruded into specific profiles that can then be screwed, cut, drilled, sawn, and sanded like ordinary wood. The properties of this composite offer alternative applications for wood where the wooden component might be exposed to external environments and weathering, because, unlike wood, it does not degrade.

This type of material is not radically new but the improved formulation of Timbercel® allows it to be extruded for applications where long continuous shapes are needed, that can then be worked as if they were wood. By changing the timber and pigments different colors can be created. Although it has not been used for any other molding technology, future development may lead to a moldable formulation.

Key Features	Fire retardant
	Durable
	Recyclable
	Good workability
	Good weatherability
More	www.britishvita.com
Typical Applications	Building and construction applications, window frames, and decking.

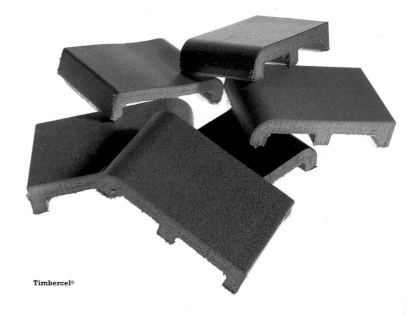

Timbercel®

Made-to-order wood grain

Alpi is a world leader in the production of reconstructed wood veneers. The key to understanding the benefits of Alpi's product over traditional wood veneers is the way in which it is produced. With natural wood grains the veneer is created by rotary-peeling thin sheets from a tree. Alpi differs in that, although it uses real wood, the grain pattern is made artificially and therefore virtually any grain, color, and design can be created.

Apart from being able to design your own veneer pattern with Alpi, the key advantage for many industries is its consistency with each leaf, which would not be possible with a natural veneer. Because it uses just two varieties of tree, Italian poplar and ayous from Cameroon, prices do not suffer from the same fluctuations as wood. Also, there are no knots, splits, or other natural flaws.

The process begins with a 2D image being produced on a CAD system, or a natural veneer is scanned. Real wood is rotary-peeled from a tree, then dyed and glued under high pressure to form a solid block in a special mold. The new veneers are sliced from the block once it has dried. The end result feels and looks like any other natural veneer and can be handled and joined in just the same way.

Dimensions	**Lengths: 2,200mm–3,400mm**
	Standard width: 620mm
	Thickness: 0.3mm–3mm; Lumber thickness: 25mm–90mm
Key Features	**Stable price**
	Low waste
	Cost-effective when compared with Burrs and Birds Eye grain patterns
	Harvesting on good forest management
	Can be replicated using trees with high growth rates
	Virtually any natural or artificial pattern can be created
	Can be used in the same way as natural veneers
More	**www.eaf.demon.co.uk**
	www.alpiwood.com
Typical Applications	**General joinery, furniture, flooring, musical instruments, doors, picture frames, and desk accessories.**

Veneer samples
Manufacturer: Alpi

Shredded wood

There are certain advantages to taking a log apart and putting it back together in a different way. Paralam is an engineered construction material made from strands of timber usually six to eight inches long, which are reconstituted and glued together to form building units. During the reforming process the weaker aspects are removed, leaving a stronger natural material with the same workability as conventional timber.

The process uses much more of the log than could be used by just sawing the tree. The strongest timber comes from the outside of the tree closest to the bark. The inner wood is young and soft. To use this part for conventional sawn timber would be impractical, as the tree would need to be cut into thin, semi-circular planks to isolate this particular wood. That's where Paralam comes in as a way of using this valuable resource.

To make Paralam, a log, typically Douglas fir or pine, is sliced into veneers which are chopped into fine fibers and mixed with glues and resins. The mixture is then heated using microwave technology, which produces a large, solid block that can be cut down into more manageable planks. This process produces a valuable construction material that makes highly efficient use of the original logs.

Key Features	Virtually no warping
	No limit to length
	Can be worked like sawn timber
	More durable than sawn timber
	Excellent dimensional stability
	Good resistance to thermal expansion
More	www.trusjoist.com
	www.lignatur.ch
Typical Applications	Beams, lintels, headers, trusses, columns, posts, decking, and railway beams.

Paralam sample
Supplier: Trusjoist

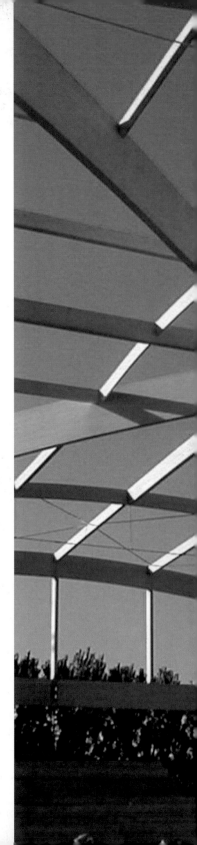

Gluing timber together to increase strength is nothing new. In the 1950s the commercial availability of a product called Glulam—an abbreviation of glued and laminated—gave architects and designers the freedom to experiment with structural timber in a way that had not been possible before.

By gluing together timbers of different thicknesses (from two layers upward) the flexibility of sawn wood is reduced and its movement is restricted. This provides a strong and stable structure, which can be made up to any size, the main restriction being dictated by transportation rather than production.

Glulam differs from board materials like plywood by using solid wood rather than veneers. The timber is laminated horizontally and can be glued to produce any curved or straight form without compromising on structural integrity. The construction uses woods of similar strengths and weight.

Reassembled

Glulam building	Key Features	Good dimensional stability
		Good strength-to-weight ratio
		Economical: the lower weight of Glulam cuts costs on foundations, transport, and erection
		Environmentally friendly
		Chemical resistance
	More	www.glulam.co.uk
		www.cwc.ca
		www.lilleheden.dk
	Typical Applications	Columns, beams, girders, trusses in interior and exterior applications, salt barns, swimming pools, and road bridges.

Biodegradable architecture

There are very few true timber gridshell buildings in existence and the Downland Gridshell workshop is the only one of its kind in the UK. Timber gridshells are rare, mainly because effective strategies for counteracting natural forces have yet to be developed, although they date back to the nineteenth century when Lamella structures were commonly used to form vaults and domes.

This large structure at The Weald and Downland Open Air Museum is a mesh of relatively thin, local, untreated oak filaments; another intelligent example of how existing materials have been used creatively. The structure is totally biodegradable and will last for approximately 100 years.

Steve Johnson explains: "A shell is a natural, extremely strong structure. A gridshell is essentially a shell with holes, but with its structure concentrated into strips. Timber gridshells have two lives. In their built incarnations, they are formful, resilient, strong objects. In their genesis stages they are perhaps more mysterious as, while being made up of stiff, woven, or overlapped linear elements, they behave more like stiff rubber than loose cloth. The particular properties of timber allow it to be deformed into a shape, and then locked."

**Weald and Downland
Gridshell Workshop
Designer: Edward Cullinan
Architects**

Key Features	**Strong structure**
	Uses local materials
	Easy to construct
	Economic use of timber
	Biodegradable
	Fire-resistant
	Resistant to fungal attack
More	**www.wealddown.co.uk**
	www.edwardcullinanarchitects.com
Typical Applications	**Shelters and trellises which eventually biodegrade leaving the plants to retain the original structure. Also used in aircraft fuselages.**

Chemical-free

The amount of twisting and bending that these woods can take before snapping defies belief. This chemical-free production method, which can transform most temperate hardwoods into Bendywood™ begins with a good quality straight-grained timber. This is steamed to plasticize the cell walls as with conventional steam bending. The now soft timber is compressed along its length with a 60-tonne hydraulic ram which causes the cell walls to compress concertina-style—it is this new structure that gives the wood its flexibility. Flexywood™, also produced by Mallinson, is permanently flexible and will not set to shape, making it an ideal timber for edging and lippings.

Sample of Bendywood™

Key Features	Flexible at room temperature
	Available in a range of temperate hardwood timbers
	Can be worked as normal timber
	Allows for easy prototyping
	Not suitable for softwoods
More	www.bendywood.com
	www.compwood.com
Typical Applications	Handrails, sports equipment, shopfittings, cabinet making, signmaking, walking sticks, door handles, curtain rails, and furniture.

Easily bent

Kerfing is the name given to dry-bending a thick section of wood. Like steam bending and laminating, it is based on a very simple principle: taking material away from a piece of timber and reducing its thickness means that it can be easily bent. The width of cuts on a kerfed board directly relates to the tightness of the final bend. The closer the spacing between the kerfs (or cuts), the tighter the radius can be.

These stools, by designer Alvar Aalto, use a laminated, kerfed bend where the grain at the end of a section is kerfed and veneers are inserted into the gaps. They illustrate Aalto's interest in exploring the possibilities of wood in furniture, which is usually a direct result of his designs for buildings. Through these experiments he revitalized the language and usage of the wood in the 1930s and developed an alternative to the fashionable Bauhaus tubular steel.

Stool 60
Designer: Alvar Aalto
Manufacturer: Artek

Dimensions	**440mm x 350mm seat diameter**
Key Features	**Allows for most timbers to be curved**
	Mass- or low-scale production
	Can be relatively simple for mock ups
More	**www.artek.fi**
Typical Applications	**Curved panels.**

Relaxed fibers

Depending on the thickness of the wood and the radius to which it is being bent, it can bend without any treatment. Until the invention of Bendywood™ and Flexywood™, the only way of bending solid timber was by kerfing or steam bending. Applying steam to a piece of wood relaxes the fibers, which allows it to be bent easily round a given form, a widely applied process that was developed by Michael Thonet in the nineteenth century.

Successful steam bending is partly dependent on choosing the right timber. The selected wood must be free of knots and shakes, and have a straight grain. Ash, beech, birch, elm, hickory, oak, walnut, and yew can all be steam bent.

This chair was designed by Marc Newson for the House of Fiction Exhibition. The soft form results from steam bending each piece of beech individually according to the radius required.

Steam-bent chair
Designer: Marc Newson
Client: House of Fiction
Exhibition

Dimensions	750mm x 750mm x 1,000mm
Key Features	Allows for bending into tight curves
	Suitable for mass- or small-scale production
	A range of woods can be used
More	www.marc-newson.com
	www.cappellini.it

Get knotted

Ever wondered how arduous and expensive spiralling. curling handrails are to make? Haldane (UK) Ltd. prides itself on putting knots into wood rather than worrying about taking them out. This handrail may look super bendy but it is actually produced by CNC-routing technology from three pieces of wood. The CNC process can cut virtually any shape from a piece of timber and is described by Managing Director Adam Forrester as, "like being handed the keys to the space shuttle when you are used to a Mini."

Investment in the new technology has paid off; Haldane can now manufacture any shape designers and architects throw at them. The full 3D machining and routing technology means designers can manufacture almost any hardwood or softwood profile. It can be used for one-offs as well as multiples of identical pieces.

Sapele timber sample

Dimensions	50mm diameter
Key Features	3D cutting technology
	Low- to high-volume production
	Can accommodate a range of materials
	Designs can be cut straight from CAD files
More	www.haldaneuk.com
Typical Applications	Glazing beads, furniture components, and handrails.

Bacteria-killing organisms

Today, toothpicks are an unremarkable, disposable addition to most kitchen cupboards. But they used to be highly valued; an essential accessory for the well-to-do and often made from ivory and silver, as well as wood.

Toothpicks are produced at a rate of 15,000 per minute, or 2.5 billion per year. The automated process begins by cutting logs into 24 three-quarter-inch blocks which are steamed to 160°F (71°C) to raise the moisture content. The logs are then sliced into veneers on a lathe and dried to remove the excess moisture. The veneers are then separated according to whether they will be used to produce flat or round toothpicks.

For round toothpicks the veneer is fed into a molding machine to produce round dowels. These are then fed into a pointing machine which consists of a series of belts and grinding stones. The picks are then polished and packed. Making flat toothpicks is a much faster process which produces up to 45,000 per minute.

So far, these valuable little stakes have not been replaced by other materials on a large scale. The natural bacteria-killing organisms in wood and its ability to soften make it the perfect material for oral hygiene.

Key Features	Heavy, dense wood
	Straight, fine-textured, and close grain
	Good for steam bending
	Good workability but can be woolly
	Can be stained and polished
More	www.diamondbrands.com
Typical Applications	Birch wood is used for toothpicks, birch plywood furniture, highly decorative veneers, general turnery, and disposable ice-cream spoons.

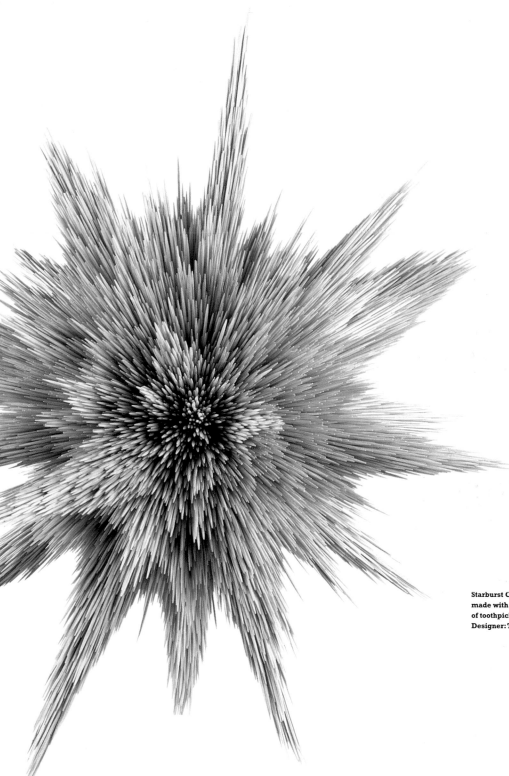

**Starburst Construction
made with thousands
of toothpicks
Designer: Tom Friedman**

Organic designs

Wood can be flexible, even curvy, when cut to thin sections and glued to a pre-existing form. Unlike working with plywood sheets, where the direction of the grain is alternated with each layer of veneer, in this type of production the grain runs in the same direction. This process has enabled organic, undulating, rhythmic forms to be produced very easily.

In 1941, Ray and Charles Eames began a series of experiments into bent laminated plywood for the Organic Design in Home Furnishing competition. They continued to develop their working methods with an order from the American Navy for 5,000 molded plywood leg splints, which led to the formation of the Plyformed Wood Company. Their use of plywood at the time fulfilled two main criteria: firstly it was economical, an important consideration just after WWII; and secondly they created forms which could be molded to the body.

The modular characteristic of the LCW chair is a result of the production of each part being addressed separately, allowing for complex and ergonomic forms to be easily produced.

LCW chair
Designers: Charles and
Ray Eames
Manufacturer: Moulded
Plywood Division, Evans

Schizzo chair
Designer: Ron Arad
Originally Manufactured
by Vitra

Key Features	Enables curves to be formed
	Can be used for low- to high-volume production
	Economical use of material
Typical Applications	Used for any shape requiring a thick, curved form.

African hardwood

Butch Smuts is a woodturner based in South Africa. He works with dense African hardwoods like lead, wild olive, and tamboti. He only uses timbers from abandoned dead trees for ecological reasons. These very hard, dense woods require special techniques for working and some pieces can take up to 17 hours to hollow.

It's rare to find a woodturner who isn't passionate about their craft and in love with their material. Some produce bowls that are never meant to function as containers, but exist only to show the natural beauty hidden beneath the bark. But it is only relatively recently that woodturning has begun to embrace the more sculptural possibilities that are detached from a formal function.

From chair and table legs to bowls and chess pieces, the ancient process of woodturning has been around for about 3,000 years. The earliest lathes were bow lathes which were simple mechanisms where the wood was held between two centers and rotated by means of cord looped around the wood and attached to a bow which was worked by either hand or foot.

Dimensions	316mm x 310mm
Key Features	Very hard and dense
	Excellent for turning
	Fine pore structure and even texture
	Not suitable for steam bending
	Difficult to work
More	www.flowgallery.co.uk
Typical Applications	Decorative veneers, interior furniture, carving, chess pieces, and musical instruments.

Red Ivory Hollow Form

Key Features	High density and tolerance
	Biodegradable, 100 percent recyclable
	Flame-resistant (fire protection class B1)
	Excellent dimensional stability
	Made from mixed waste products without producing new waste
	High resistance to damp compared to fiberboard or MDF
More	www.fasalex.com
	www.strandex.com
Typical Applications	Cable channels, skirting boards, replacements for extruded plastic and long-profiled wooden shapes, electrical conduits, and replacements for PVC on window frames.

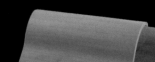

Sliding chair
Designer: Yann Gafsou

Intelligent material

"At the beginning of this project my wish was to study twentieth-century furniture design; to become more acquainted with the past in order to understand the present and the future. From Breuer's Wassily chair to Alvar Aalto's Number 43, these designs all exploited a new process, a local know-how, demonstrating properties of new materials at the same time. From then on, I really wanted to use a material as a guideline on this project; I wanted to let the material and the process guide me to an outcome," says Yann Gafsou.

This is the rationale behind Gafsou's extruded wooden chair, made from what he describes as, "a material for the twenty-first century." It is ecological, economical, and new. The design uses local waste materials and the manufacturing process produces no waste. As well as combining the manufacturing properties of plastics with the workability of wood, this material is also biodegradable and not restricted to wood fibers. Rice, soya beans, bamboo, straw, and even peanuts can be used as a base. And if you are after a particular wood effect you can specify it as one of the many finishes available.

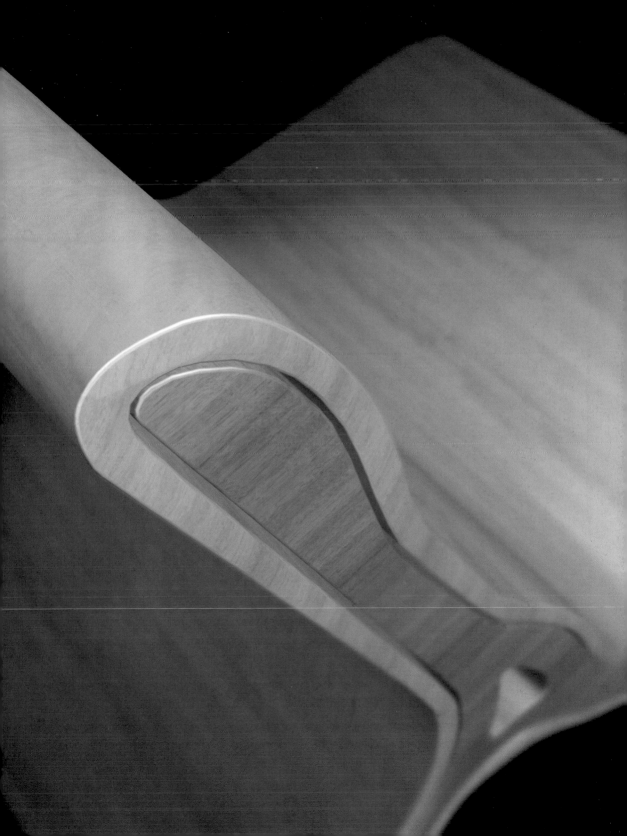

Borrowed technology

Layering wood for the watertight construction of boats has been developed and practiced by craftsmen throughout history. But the Mussel bathtub is made of wood which has been treated to keep the water in rather than out.

The final design is based on two years of development by designers and boat builders, and applies construction techniques specific to boat building. The technology involves glass-reinforced plastic over which small pieces of 3mm saw-cut veneer are formed. The wooden bath heightens the sensual experience of bathtime by providing a pleasant aroma as well as a tactile, warm surface to lie against.

Dimensions	**240mm x 1,500mm**
Key Features	**Rigid construction**
	Lightweight structure
	Oil and varnish provide watertight construction
	Versatile production method
More	**www.gnausch.de**
Typical Applications	**Yacht construction.**

Bademuschel bathtub
Designer: Tilo Gnausch

Wood is not generally thought of as a mass-production material. Plastic definitely, glass and metal for sure, but wood does not have a history of being exploited to make millions of identical products. However, the match is an interesting exception.

Matches are generally made from aspen and poplar. First the wood is cut into sheets of veneer which are chopped into square splints and fed into a series of holes within metal plates. These plates carry the matches through the various stages of production: the next being a dip in a chemical bath to prevent afterglow. They are then taken through paraffin to help them burn more easily. Lastly, the heads are applied. Machines can yield approximately 50 million matches per day.

Key Features	Coarse texture
	Rich, straight grain
	Good workability and finishing
	Good resistance to water
	Excellent for steam bending
Typical Applications	Furniture, flooring, boat building, wine and whiskey barrels, frames, doors, panelling, church pews, and carving.

50 million per day

Index

010 photo by Xavier Young; 011 Rado; 013 Ceram Technology, photo by Xavier Young; 014015 Head UK; 016017 CEVP; 018019 Nacsound; 020 Sorma; 021 KC Lo; 022023 Hering-Berlin; 024025 Droog Design; 026 Héctor Serrano; 027 Gallery Kreo; 028029 Kathryn Hearn, photo by Andrew Watson; 030031 Twenty Twenty-One; 032033 Hella Jongerius; 034 KC Lo; 035 Satyendra Pakhalé, photo by Corné Bastiaansen; 036037 Victoria Rothschild and Anna Usborne; 038039 Kelvin J. Birk; 040 Satyendra Pakhalé, photo by Corné Bastiaansen; 041 Royal Doulton; 042 Laser Cutting UK; 043 Wade Ceramics, photo by Xavier Young; 044045 Ceram Technology, photo by Xavier Young; 046047 HG Matthews, photo by Xavier Young; 048049 3M, photo by Xavier Young; 050051 3M, photo by Xavier Young; 052 Magnet Applications, photo by Xavier Young; 053 Precision Ceramics, photo by Xavier Young; 054055 UK General Hybrid, photo by Xavier Young; 058059 Amy Cushing; 060 Design House, Stockholm; 061 Jukka Isotalo; 062063 Fusion Glass Designs Ltd.; 064 photo by Xavier Young; 065 photo by Xavier Young; 066067 Langfords & Co. and Norton Cowan Communications; 068 photo by Xavier Young; 069 Paul McClarin, photo by Xavier Young; 070071 Rocco Borghese; 072 Marco Sousa Santos and Proto Design; 073 Gijs Bakker Design; 074075 photo by Xavier Young; 076 photo by Xavier Young; 077 Aldo Bakker; 078 3M; 079 photo by Xavier Young; 080 photo by Xavier Young; 081 NASA; 082 Pilkington Glass; 083 Corning; 084 Saint Gobain; 085 Solar Century, Big Brother house photo by Trish Littler; 086087 Jhan Stanley; 088 Rebecca Newnham, photo by David Bird; 089 John Blazy; 090091 Schott; 092 Cellbond Composites Ltd.; 093 Ruth Spaak; 094095 Foster and Partners, photo by Nigel Young; 096097 Vitglass; 098 Mosaik and Pierre Mesguish, photo by Xavier Young; 099 Thomas Heatherwick Studio; 100 Michael Anastassiades; 101 Chris Lefteri; 102 Gruppe RE; 103 Architectural Window Films, photo by Rodney Harrigan; 106107 Con Edison and Karim Rashid; 108 Stelton and Arne Jacobsen; 109 Skultuna Messingsbruk and Olof Kolte Design; 110 OMK Design and Rodney Kinsman; 111 OMK Design and Rodney Kinsman; 112113 Nambe and Karim Rashid; 114115 Purves & Purves and Ben Panayi, photo by Xavier Young; 116 Full Blown Metals and Stephen Newby, photo by Joseph Hutt; 117 Sam Buxton; 118119 Lemark, photo by Xavier Young; 120 BJS Electroforming; 121 Memory-Metalle GmbH; 122123 Alusion, photo by Xavier Young; 124125 Materials and Aerospace Corporation, photo by Xavier Young; 126127 Corus Space; 128129 Ingo Maurer; 130131 Audi; 132 LINDBERG; 133 Superform Aluminum and Ron Arad; 134 Ted Noten; 135 Issey Miyake; 136 Idaho, Tom Longhurst, and Simon Proctor; 137 Charisma; 138139 Jean Nouvel and GIMM Architekten; 140 Clauss Markisen and Projeckt GmbH; 141 Gebr Kufferath AG; 142 Boris Bally, photo by J. W. Johnson; 143 Blu Dot.

John Christakos, Charles Lazor, and Maurice Blanks; 144145 BJS Electroforming, photo by Stuart Graham; 146147 Afroditi Krassa; 148149 Maglite and Anthony Maglica, photo by Xavier Young; 150151 photo by Xavier Young; 152153 Jeff Rowland and Vertec Tool; 156 The Federal Reserve Bank of Australia, photo by Xavier Young; 157 Miller Brewing Company, photo by Xavier Young; 158 Smile Plastics, photo by Xavier Young; 159 Stewart Grant/Katz Collection; 160161 Tom Dixon; 162 Cellbond Composites Ltd.; 163 photo by Xavier Young; 164165 Chromazone; 166 photo by Xavier Young; 167 Carolina Herrera, New York; 168 Plank, 169 Ronan & Erwan Bouroullec; 170 Flexplay; 171 photo by Xavier Young; 172173 Foampartner; 174 photo by Xavier Young; 175 VICTORINOX; 176177 Herman Miller; 178 photo by Xavier Young; 179 Alessi; 180181 Maaike Evers and Mike Simonian; 182183 Rob Thompson; 184185 photo by Xavier Young; 186 photo by Xavier Young; 187 Plantic; 188 Hugo Jamson; 189 photo by Xavier Young; 190191 Tom Dixon; 192193 photo by Xavier Young; 194 Barbara Schmidt; 195 photo by Thomas Duval; 196 Omlet Ltd.; 197 photo by Xavier Young; 198199 Karim Rashid; 200201 photo by Xavier Young; 202 Nike Inc.; 203 photo by Xavier Young; 204205 Yves Béhar; 208 Philipp Mainzer; 209 KC Lo; 210 Gijs Bakker; 211 Modern Garden Furniture Company; 212213 Hans Sandgren Jakobsen; 214 John Makepeace; 215 David Landess; 216217 Gill Wilson and the One Tree Project, photo by Robert Walker; 218 Marti Gruixé and Droog Design; 219 photo by Xavier Young; 220221 Melissa Harbour, photo by Daniel Hennessy; 222 Giovanni Sacchi; 223 James Smith; 224 photo by Xavier Young; 225 John Makepeace; 226227 Dunkelman & Sons, photo by Xavier Young; 228 Thor Hammer; 229 Ricardo Blumer; 230231 photo by Xavier Young; 232 photo by Xavier Young; 233 photo by Xavier Young; 234 photo by Xavier Young; 235 Alpi; 236237 Trus Joist, photo by Xavier Young; 238239 Glued Laminated Timber Association; 240241 The Weald and Downland Open Air Museum; 242 Mallinson; 243 Alvar Aalto, 244 Marc Newson; 245 Haldane (UK) Ltd.; 246247 photo by Xavier Young; 248 LCW chair: Charles and Ray Eames. © 2002 Eames Office, Schizzo chair: Ron Arad; 249 photo by Xavier Young; 250251 Yann Gafsou; 252 Tilo Gnausch; 253 photo by Xavier Young

Credits